EGYPTIAN BIRTH SIGNS

EGYPTIAN BIRTH SIGNS

THE SECRETS OF THE ANCIENT EGYPTIAN HOROSCOPE

Storm Constantine

Thorsons

Thorsons
An Imprint of HarperCollins*Publishers*
77–85 Fulham Palace Road
Hammersmith, London W6 8JB

The Thorsons website is:
www.thorsons.com

and *Thorsons*

are trademarks of
HarperCollins*Publishers* Limited.

Published by Thorsons 2002

10 9 8 7 6 5 4 3 2 1

© Storm Constantine and Graham S. Phillips 2001

Storm Constantine and Graham S. Phillips assert the moral right
to be identified as the authors of this work

A catalogue record for this book
is available from the British Library

ISBN 0–00–713138–0

© Chris Down - illustrations

Printed and bound in Great Britain by
Martins the Printers, Berwick upon Tweed

CONTENTS

Introduction   vii

Chapter 1	Thoth	29 August–27 September	1
Chapter 2	Horus	28 September–27 October	20
Chapter 3	Wadjet	28 October–26 November	40
Chapter 4	Sekhmet	27 November–26 December	60
Chapter 5	The Sphinx	27 December–25 January	80
Chapter 6	Shu	26 January–24 February	99
Chapter 7	Isis	25 February–26 March	118
Chapter 8	Osiris	27 March–25 April	137
Chapter 9	Amun	26 April–25 May	157
Chapter 10	Hathor	26 May–24 June	177
Chapter 11	The Phoenix	25 June–24 July	197
Chapter 12	Anubis	25 July–28 August	216

Resources   235

INTRODUCTION

Very little is known about Egyptian astrology except for one
surviving design (or *stela*) discovered on the ceiling in the Temple of
Hathor at Dendera in central Egypt. Now in the Louvre in Paris, this
12-inch stone disc was probably made around 50 BC, which was the
end of the period known as the New Kingdom, the time of
Cleopatra, when the Romans annexed Egypt to their empire. The
artefact from Dendera shows that the zodiac was divided into 18
constellations represented by various animals. However, unlike the
later Greeks, from whom we have inherited our present astrological
signs, the Egyptians did not use these zodiac constellations for natal
astrology. Their birth signs were determined by the Egyptian months
of the year. The richly decorated stela of Dendera also shows the
deities and creatures that presided over the months.

There are a number of different versions of the Egyptian calendar,
but the one used for this book derives from the end of Ancient
Egyptian history. At different periods throughout their history, the
Egyptians altered the time of their new year and the start of each
month. In the Old Kingdom, (2686–2181 BC) the year began on the

Spring Equinox (21 March). Thus, the 12 months would each run (roughly) from the 21st–20th.

After various political upheavals, the Middle Kingdom began in 2040 BC and lasted until 1782 BC. During this time, the New Year coincided with the heliacal rising of the star Sirius (known in Egyptian as Sothis), which occurred in mid-July, so the months also began round about what is now the 15th of the month in our modern calendar. Also, beliefs and systems varied around the country, so during the Middle Kingdom, some areas stuck to the original calendar. There were also local variations on the deities associated with each month.

Because the early calendar followed a lunar cycle, as the years passed, they eventually became slightly 'out', so to remedy this, five extra, or 'epagomenal' days were added, to keep the years in line. They were placed between what is now 14–18 July. This, of course, is similar to our modern 'leap year', when an extra day is added to February every four years. The epagomenal days were seen as holy and the birthdays of particularly important gods, who were the children of the god Geb (the earth) and the goddess Nut (the sky). Although this legend and its symbols are not examined in depth in this system, as it relates to an earlier calendar than the one used here, they might be of special interest to those born on the same dates. The table below indicates which were the birthdays of which deities:

14 July   Osiris, Lord of the Underworld, and one of the most important gods.

15 July   Horus the Elder, a falcon god (not to be confused with Osiris' own son of the same name, who presides over the months September to October)

16 July   Set, a god of chaotic forces, who was regarded with great veneration.

17 July   Isis, one of the premier goddesses of Ancient Egypt, regarded as 'great in magic'. She became the wife of Osiris.

18 July   Nephthys. She became the wife of Set, but in legend also had a child with Osiris – the jackal-headed god, Anubis.

By the Late Kingdom, it had become firmly established that the year began with the inundation of the Nile on 29 August. By this time, the calendar had become more fully worked out, and the Dendera zodiac was crafted during this period.

The Egyptian year was always divided into three seasons of four months, rather than our four seasons of three months. Because of their climate, the Egyptians did not have a winter as we do. Their seasons were the Inundation, when the River Nile overflowed its banks and fertilized the land with rich, dark soil, the Growing Season, when the people farmed the land and the Harvest Season, when the crops were gathered in, and the year came to its blistering, parched close before the Inundation began the cycle again. Each of the 12 months of the year was ruled over by a different god or sacred creature. From inscriptions at the Temple of Hathor, we know that these divinities were thought to influence a person's physical and mental attributes, just as today's zodiac signs are thought to determine one's personality and appearance. However, to date, no hieroglyphic inscriptions have been found to provide specific details concerning the characteristics of each sign.

This book attempts to reconstruct the characteristics of these Egyptian birth signs. From computer analysis of hundreds of volunteers who completed a detailed questionnaire about themselves, it was possible to determine the characteristics shared by those born in each Egyptian sign. From this survey it has been viable to do what has not been done for 2000 years – present a modern interpretation of the Egyptian birth signs.

Many people are fascinated by Ancient Egypt and feel drawn to its exotic spirituality. The gods themselves, mysterious creatures of sometimes bizarre appearance, inspire the imagination. We can find strength in the image of lioness-headed Sekhmet, lady of power and fire, and a lusty joy for life in the goddess of love, Hathor, who was sometimes depicted as a cow, although she was mostly represented in art as a beautiful woman. Jackal-headed Anubis is the weigher of hearts, while Ibis-headed Thoth presides over writing and wisdom. Each of the deities who govern the months of the year has particular characteristics and attributes. It could be said they have an 'essence', which flavours the month itself.

As well as character and relationships analysis, you'll also find other information in each chapter, such as which stones, flowers, herbs, etc. are relevant to each sign. These correspondences are not drawn from Western astrology, but from the ancient system of the Tree of Life or Cabbala. The Cabbala was certainly used by the ancient Israelites but, more importantly in this case, modern archaeological discoveries made at Amarna in Central Egypt have suggested that this ancient magical system originated with the mysterious Egyptian pharaoh, Akhenaten. As the Cabbala provides a sensible and comprehensive 'map' of the universe and the human psyche, it seemed most appropriate to use this system as a basis for the sign correspondences.

At the end of each chapter, you'll also find a small 'working'. This is like a prayer or invocation that calls upon the 'flavour' of the month, the god or goddess who presides over it. You can commune with the deity of your particular sign at any time. For example, if you are a 'Thoth', born between 29 August and 27 September, you could perform the small working whenever you feel in need of calling upon Thoth's divine help, for protection or inspiration. Thoth's energy is of particular importance to creative people, journalists or writers. But what if you weren't born in his sign? You can still ask Thoth for help, but preferably at the time of year when his influence is strongest, i.e. the month over which he rules. Thus, you can perform any of the workings, regardless of which sign you were born under.

For example, between the dates of 28 September and 27 October, the presiding deity is Horus. During this time, you can perform the Horus working to call upon his help, no matter what sign you are yourself. The deities have particular 'specialities', which sometimes might be of significance to you, but it's important to remember that all the gods and goddesses share the qualities of protection and helpfulness, and can be called upon whenever you need their strength.

To perform a working, look at the correspondences for the sign. If we use Thoth as an example again, make sure you have the appropriate stone, flower, herb, etc. you need and construct a small altar by arranging these items around a central orange candle (Thoth's colour). Coffee tables make particularly good altars! The Ancient Eygptians made offerings to their deities of food they believed the gods particularly liked. In keeping with this idea, place a relevant offering of food (in this case, a segmented orange), arranged in a small dish or bowl on your altar. The gods were also supposed to be extremely fond of perfume, so you should burn a scented oil, incense or joss stick of the pertinent flavour. Bark, leaves, fruit or flowers of Thoth's personal tree can also be included in your altar arrangement. If you're unable to gather all these items, don't worry, just use as many as you can. Choose an incense flavour closest to the one given in the correspondences. Correspondences were very important to Ancient Egyptian priests. They believed that things of like colour or flavour shared the same magical properties, so you can use any orange flower if that's all you can get.

You can add as many personal touches to the altar as you like, including a small statue of the deity (if you have one) or else a picture of him. (The hieroglyphic symbols for the gods that appear in each chapter can be used as templates, which you can copy.) You can use an altar cloth of the pertinent colour or place other items upon it that you feel are appropriate – for example, ornaments, feathers or stones of Thoth's colour.

When you are ready, sit comfortably before your altar. Have some soft music playing in the background that seems right for the occasion. Breathe deeply and slowly for a minute or so with your eyes closed. This helps alter your state of consciousness, so you're in the right, meditative frame of mind. Then, read out the prayer to Thoth. When you have finished, you can eat a segment of the orange, if you like. It is said that the gods can experience earthly pleasures through humans, so it's like giving Thoth a taste of the fruit. Make an offering of what is left by casting it out over your garden, or some other patch of earth, for wild animals to consume.

The prayers for each sign have the same basic framework. I do not suggest they are word-for-word facsimiles of invocations used by Egyptian priests, but I have used known titles for the gods, and in some cases, literal Egyptian translations of some of those titles. In other cases, the use of an Egyptian-English dictionary provided the inspiration I needed. Basically, I took the information I had and expanded upon it, using my imagination. This is something you can do yourself too. If you want to, you can expand upon the given prayer to include particular things for which you would like help or inspiration. The most important aspect of doing work of this kind is the amount of your will and intention you put into it.

When you do a magical working, you are putting out your intentions into the universe, making a connection with the source of all, whether you believe that's a mass of formless energy or a god or goddess. Gods are the masks worn by the universal life energy, so that we, as humans, can understand it and give it a face. Presented in this book are some of the more exotic faces of this energy, and I hope that in understanding a little of them so you will come to understand more about yourself.

Storm Constantine, 2001.

CHAPTER 1

• THOTH •

29 AUGUST–27 SEPTEMBER

O great Thoth, lord of the mind and guardian of learning, you are the bringer of knowledge to mankind.

From a first-century papyrus discovered in Alexandria.

The Ibis-headed god Thoth was the lord of the moon, and his name in Ancient Egyptian was Tehuti. He was the lord of time and the god of learning and imagination, presiding over scribes and knowledge. Accordingly, those born in this sign share an unusual combination of both the materialistic and the imaginative. One of the chief characteristics of the Thoth personality is to constantly question the world about them. They are both analytical and self-critical, sometimes to the extent of impeding progress. However, the Thoth can achieve remarkable results in a very short time.

In social circumstances the Thoth is often the one to initiate, plan and organize events. However, they can sometimes be a problem to others. Their interests can be so varied that they will change horses in mid stream and those who may have dropped everything to follow them can be left high and dry. This is not because they are insensitive: they naturally assume that others will be like themselves and update their interests if something more appropriate comes along. However, when they are working professionally on behalf of others, the Thoth's altruism means that they will see a task through to its conclusion to the very best of their ability.

Although the Thoth may express a keen interest in the arts, they rarely enjoy concerts or theatre, becoming restless when forced to remain seated for any length of time. Their own interests being original, they enjoy mental rather than physical pastimes. Thoth people seldom join societies, preferring to create their own amusement. Thoths are reluctant leaders, usually preferring to go it alone. Blessed with an abundance of mental energy, they are capable of handling most tasks that befall them. They also have the enviable capacity to land on their feet should a crisis occur.

POSITIVE CHARACTERISTICS

The Thoth has great versatility. Endowed with an alert mind and an excellent memory, they are capable of solving many problems that others find difficult. They are especially precise regarding minute detail. Neat and methodical, they take pride in their work. In business, they work best alone, being capable of long periods of devoted activity. Philosophical interests are a marked feature, with considerable originality of ideas.

NEGATIVE CHARACTERISTICS

If an enterprise fails the Thoth may become oversensitive and quick to take offence. Pessimism is usual for a Thoth who has suffered a setback and the response is generally to withdraw, accepting further problems as if they somehow deserve them. Although critical of themselves, they dislike being criticized by others and are usually the last people to take advice. Extravagance and impatience can lead to financial problems.

APPEARANCE

Thoth people usually have an upright appearance, smooth complexion with warm, attractive eyes. Often large, the eyes are commonly the most striking feature of the Thoth. They tend to be slim with sharp or angular features. Usually they retain a youthful appearance well into middle age. Even the worry lines that are likely to appear on their faces make them look wiser rather than older.

HEALTH

The parts of the body readily prone to infection are the stomach and abdomen; indigestion and intestinal difficulties are invariably complaints of this group. Nervous disorders may also be in evidence and hypochondria is common. Leave them to browse through a medical dictionary and before long they think they're coming down with everything under the sun. Strangely enough, the Thoth is often the bravest sign when it comes to genuine illness. If they do fall sick or face injury, they cope well and may even continue with their normal routine against medical advice. However, Thoth is a sign of good health and those born in this cycle are usually fit and trim.

WORDS OF ADVICE

As this is a sign of versatility, the Thoth should remain focused on one job at a time, rather than numerous problems simultaneously. Their greatest drawback is that they have too many interests, ideas, and skills to devote themselves sufficiently to a single project. Their hypercritical side badly needs controlling, as does their touchiness about being criticised themselves. Extremely sensitive to criticism, the Thoth is often distracted or dissuaded by adverse opinion. They should concentrate more on what they are doing and worry less about what others may think. They must also learn to control the desire to overspend. Although their generosity is admirable, extravagance is always a risk. More than any other sign, money burns a hole in the Thoth's pocket.

SUITABLE OCCUPATIONS

Writing professions, such as journalism, can be ideal for the Thoth as those born in this sign have inquiring and critical minds. Indeed, in Egyptian mythology Thoth was the scribe of the gods. Being natural entertainers, acting or performing of any kind can be a fitting career for the Thoth. They can also become accomplished musicians. Their outgoing personality and highly developed social skills also makes those born in this sign ideally suited for careers in sales or public relations. In fact, their eloquence coupled with a flair for the dramatic makes the Thoth an excellent representative for the causes of others and so lawyers, agents and entertainment managers are often born in this sign. As Thoth was also the god of learning, men and women of this sign can make excellent teachers and lecturers, with inventive ways of making their subject matter interesting for students.

THE THOTH AT WORK

Thoths are practical, industrious and conscientious about their work, being particularly methodical in the way they go about it. Walking encyclopaedias, the Thoth's hobbies are often related to their jobs. The Thoth's inability to relax means that, where possible, they take their work home with them. They have no intention of knocking off the moment the working day ends. Unlike signs who find the thought of after-hours work disagreeable, the Thoth usually enjoys it. The Thoth works best in short, sharp bursts, however, and dislikes being tied down to rules and regulations.

THE THOTH WOMAN

You will not catch a Thoth woman slopping around the house in a tracksuit or dressing gown. She always appears immaculate from the moment the day begins. Her home will be tastefully furnished and uncluttered, with a preference for light, open and airy rooms. The only cluttered place in her home will be her medicine cupboard which is likely to be crammed with bottles of pills and a well-stocked first-aid kit. Like their male counterparts, Thoth women tend to be hypochondriacs.

Thoth women are practical and realistic regarding relationships. They never expect too much and are prepared to work towards a long and happy marriage. If a relationship fails, however, they are well prepared to move on, providing they know that the situation is really hopeless. Seldom holding grudges, the Thoth woman does not infer rejection from the break-up of a relationship and copes well with matrimonial problems.

THE THOTH MAN
Although somewhat fussy or faddy, the Thoth man is a good socializer. At ease in the company of both sexes, he has an entertaining sense of humour and a versatile character, making him the soul of any party. However, the Thoth often gives the impression that he is not quite sharing the spirit of the occasion. Not that he appears rude or disinterested; rather, he is usually thinking of more than one thing at once.

In domestic life the Thoth man is neat and tidy, unable to concentrate if he is surrounded by muddle. He makes a good husband for the woman who wants her partner to do their fair share of the housework. Taking great care to get to know his prospective partner well before plunging into marriage, the Thoth is usually faithful in a relationship, making certain that one has ended before another begins. He will not shirk his obligations to an ex-partner, neither will he knowingly be responsible for breaking up someone else's marriage.

THE THOTH PARENT
Thoths make good parents and take a keen interest in their children's education. They bring up their children with concern and kindness, are seldom strict and refrain from any form of punishment unless absolutely necessary. The Thoth treats the child as they would treat an adult, always prepared to explain why something should be done in a particular way. Indeed, Thoths set their children a good example with their tidy habits and considerate manners.

THE THOTH CHILD
Thoths can be difficult children. Although they seldom find themselves in serious trouble, or have a negative attitude to life, the

Thoth child is hyperactive. They rarely sit still and are always inquisitive. They are forever inventing new games to play and sometimes they will even break a toy to modify it for some other purpose. Their creative imagination earns them many friends but often leads to quarrels with parents or elders. In short, the Thoth child can be extremely tiring.

Thoth children are hardly ever rude and are perhaps the most polite young people of any sign. Unfortunately, their sense of humour can get them into trouble, even though their pranks are not deliberately destructive, cruel or malicious. Paradoxically, the same good-humoured jesting by the Thoth adult often results in considerable popularity. At school, the Thoth child may have the ability to be top of the class, although they are often distracted by their restless nature. 'Has the ability to do much better' or 'fools around in class' are often the words on their school reports. However, although they may not do so well during term time, when it comes to examinations the Thoth invariably makes up for it, being capable of intense revising.

THE THOTH FRIEND

Thoths are generous and entertaining friends. Never short of new ideas, they are fun to be with: perhaps the best people with whom to share a night out. They are also a mine of information, having so many varied interests and experiences that they can keep you engrossed for hours. They have good manners and never cause embarrassment in mixed company.

Sometimes, however, Thoths can be a trial. You may be feeling tired, or in need of peace and quiet, and along comes the Thoth with another great idea. Thoths just can't relax: they have to keep busy, and see to it that you too are kept on the go. Although they have the best of intentions, there are times when the Thoth will be critical of their friends, expecting too much of others. However, Thoths offer constructive advice. All the same, it must be acknowledged that Thoths are hair-splitters, and quibble over minor matters of no real consequence.

Loyal though they are to their nearest and dearest, they are clear sighted about the shortcomings of relatives, partners and close friends — and quick to remind them. Nevertheless, the common good is usually a high priority for the Thoth, who is prepared to make many a personal sacrifice to help those around them.

THE THOTH PARTNER

One of the strangest Thoth traits is their failure to realise when they are attractive to a member of the opposite sex. It usually comes as a complete shock when they discover that someone is interested in them. This is often taken to be a lack of interest on the Thoth's part – a common and sometimes sad mistake. The Thoth man is particularity shy when it comes to starting a relationship, which is due to their own self-criticism rather than a lack of confidence. Although they worry too much and sometimes fail to act, Thoth men and women are generally caring and emotionally uninhibited once they have found the right partner.

Whether attractive or plain, both male and female Thoths have an entertaining personality that often appeals to the opposite sex. However, Thoths are usually bound up with their careers and are in no hurry to marry.

Relationships are sometimes made difficult by an obstinate spirit. There is a marked tendency to disregard the attitudes of others or offend without intent. The Thoth needs to consider every angle of a problem, which so often leads to too much preparation and not enough action. Frequently, Thoths fail to seize opportunities offered them on a plate. Once they have found something to which they are committed, Thoth commitment is usually total. The good-natured and accommodating Thoth should not be mistaken as compliant. Those who consider the Thoth a pushover are in for a shock.

THOTH AND OTHER SIGNS

AFFINITY SIGNS
ANUBIS AND HATHOR: The Thoth particularly enjoys the company of the Anubis and Hathor. Hathor's romanticism makes them an eager audience for the imaginative ideas of the Thoth. The Anubis is also imaginative and together they inspire one another.

THE PHOENIX: Thoth is a mood-swinger and their behaviour can be erratic. Unlike many signs, the Phoenix is almost impervious to the emotional swings of others. As both the Phoenix and the Thoth need their own space, they make excellent partners and long-lasting relationships are possible.

THOTH: Thoth generally works best with other Thoths. Thoth creativity can develop the Thoth's ideas, while two Thoths complement each other in business matters.

PROBLEM SIGNS

OSIRIS AND WADJET: Osiris and Wadjet are generally signs where the Thoth finds greatest difficulty. Both leadership signs, they enjoy taking charge too much for Thoth's liking. Osiris is often too bossy, while Wadjet – in the Thoth's opinion – is far too inquisitive.

THE SPHINX: The Sphinx is the sign that the Thoth finds hardest to fathom. Their ability to make something out of nothing, and their keen financial sense, are mysteries to the Thoth.

AMUN: The Amun likes consistency. The Thoth enjoys a far too erratic life style for the Amun.

OTHER SIGNS

HORUS: Although the Horus can make a good acquaintance, being inspired by the Thoth, they do not necessarily make ideal partners. The Thoth lacks the romantic affection that the Horus needs.

SEKHMET: Sekhmet's optimism and will to succeed is admired by the Thoth, although they may become frustrated by the Sekhmet's abrupt changes of plans and failure to see the obvious.

SHU: The Thoth is often attracted to the openness of the Shu, although the Thoth can mentally exhaust the Shu who prefers a more serene lifestyle.

ISIS: Although the Isis and the Thoth mix well socially, relationships or business partnerships can suffer. When together, they tend to behave irresponsibly.

FATE AND FORTUNE

Over the course of the year the Thoth can expect the following influences to affect their lives during the separate Egyptian months:

THOTH 29 AUGUST – 27 SEPTEMBER:

During their own sign the Thoth is at their most self-critical. They may be inclined to concede defeat rather too readily. Relationships and friendships may suffer due to Thoth self-recrimination.

HORUS 28 SEPTEMBER – 27 OCTOBER:

The month of Horus, more than any other sign, is a time of new opportunities in romantic or adventurous affairs for the Thoth. It is often their most successful month in any endeavour and new opportunities are likely. Thoth people are frequently inspired and quick to seize the initiative at this time of year.

WADJET 28 OCTOBER – 26 NOVEMBER:

The Wadjet serpent can open many unexpected doors in the Thoth's life. Even if problems do occur the Thoth is well placed to divert them to their advantage.

SEKHMET 27 NOVEMBER – 26 DECEMBER:

The month of the Sekhmet is a cycle of high activity for the Thoth. They should be careful not to overwork themselves. Thoth people can become touchy or oversensitive to the opinions of others. The Thoth may need to spend time alone during the Sekhmet month.

THE SPHINX 27 DECEMBER – 25 JANUARY:

The Thoth is generally extravagant by nature. During the month of the Sphinx they tend to spend more than they should. It is also a time that the Thoth throws caution to the wind. The Thoth loves a mystery, and the riddle of the Sphinx may prove disastrous if attempted but unsolved. An accepted challenge may well backfire at this time of the year. Caution is certainly the better of valour for the Thoth during the month of the Sphinx.

SHU 26 JANUARY – 24 FEBRUARY:

In Egyptian mythology Shu was a god of good fortune. This is particularly true for the Thoth. During this month most Thoths find that something long awaited will finally materialize. Any Thoth seeking fresh romantic attachments may find this month particularly eventful.

ISIS 25 FEBRUARY – 26 MARCH:

Isis is specifically a sign of love and romance as far as the Thoth is concerned. Successful Thoth relationships are so often formed during the month of Isis.

OSIRIS 27 MARCH – 25 APRIL:

Strangely, the month of Osiris is often a time when the Thoth bumps into people they prefer not to meet. It can also be a time of unwelcome news and upset plans. Many Thoths will not be unhappy when the cycle of Osiris is complete.

AMUN 26 APRIL – 25 MAY:

During the month of Amun many Thoth people will be ready for something different in their lives. New opportunities, particularly in social circumstances, are likely. It is also a favourable time for romance.

HATHOR 26 MAY – 24 JUNE:

During the month of Hathor the Thoth is particularly astute in their approach to most endeavours. It is a time of sound judgement, and many Thoths will benefit from important decisions made during this cycle. This is their luckiest month for anything involving chance.

THE PHOENIX 25 JUNE – 24 JULY:

The Thoth, being a particularly analytical and self-critical sign, can be too cautious in this month. Thoths are likely to change their mind repeatedly during this cycle. It is probably the best time of year to take a vacation.

ANUBIS 25 JULY – 28 AUGUST:

For the Thoth, Anubis is the message bearer and good news is likely. If the Thoth is considering a change of home or occupation, now can be a favourable time to start looking.

THOTH CORRESPONDENCES

STONE   CARNELIAN
TREE   QUINCE
FOOD   ORANGE
HERB   THYME
FLOWER   MARIGOLD

COLOUR   ORANGE
LUCKY NUMBER 8
INCENSE   LAVENDER
ANIMAL   IBIS
SYMBOL

FAMOUS THOTHS

Cameron Diaz, Liam Gallagher, Hugh Grant, Prince Harry, Stephen King, Sam Neill, Keanu Reeves, H.G. Wells.

THOTH WORKING

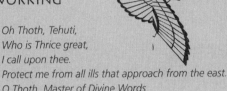

Oh Thoth, Tehuti,
Who is Thrice great,
I call upon thee.
Protect me from all ills that approach from the east.
O Thoth, Master of Divine Words
Protect me from all ills that approach from the south.
Tehuti, Lord of Truth.

Protect me from all ills that approach from the west.
Great Thoth, Scribe of the Gods
Protect me from from all ills that approach from the north.
Oh Thoth, Who is Mighty in Speech
Remain at all times about me
O Tehuti pa aa, pa aa, pa aa.
Lord of the Sacred Words
When I cannot hear, lead me
Lord of Khemennu, Self-Created
When I cannot see, show me the way.
Guardian of the Sacred Books in the House of the Life
Let me recognize and seize the opportunities that
*   I am granted.*

Let thy hand work through me.
Guide me to my path of destiny.
Grant me now thy power.
Tehuti, pa aa, pa aa, pa aa.

CHAPTER 2

• HORUS •

28 SEPTEMBER–27 OCTOBER

*I am the lord of the morning sun. I am one
who is with the sound eye; even when closed
I am in its protection.*

From the Egyptian Book of the Dead.

The falcon-headed god Horus (whose name in Ancient Egyptian was
Heru), was the son of Osiris and Isis and god of the rising sun. He
was a symbol of divine kingship and risked his very existence to
avenge his father's death and oppose his slayer, Set. During the
battle between the two gods Horus lost an eye that, it is said,
became a precious stone – the ultimate talisman of protection,

resurrection and eternal life. Like their mythical counterpart, those born in the sign of Horus often take risks or embark upon enterprises without taking precautions. When the risks pay off, however, great success is possible. The Horus is stubborn in their convictions although they make loyal and trustworthy friends. Like the lost talisman, the Eye of Horus, this is a sign of protection, and those born in this cycle are usually highly protective of those they love.

The Horus loves variety and is always prepared for a new challenge. They have extreme confidence in all endeavours and so disasters are seldom anticipated. Being so inventive, those born in this sign tend to be absent-minded and are forever losing their personal possessions or mislaying important items. Although at their best during a difficult, up-hill struggle, the Horus finds it hard to start again if disaster should strike.

Horus people are essentially good-natured and considerate. They are motivated by the urge to extract the best from life, as much by adapting themselves to existing conditions as by creating new possibilities. Horus people, however, do not attempt to bulldoze their way through obstacles but skilfully navigate their way around them. In Egyptian mythology Horus was the protector of the animal kingdom and, like their mythical counterpart, many born in this cycle have a strong affinity with living creatures of all kinds.

POSITIVE CHARACTERISTICS

Those born in this cycle are inventive and creative, having equal artistic and technical flair. Always on the look out for something new, they are prepared to take risks courageously. Not easily distracted, those born in the Horus sign have an optimistic attitude towards most endeavours. They share an emotional and romantic temperament, coupled with a keen interest in the well-being of others. The Horus is blessed with an abundance of originality and lets little stand in the way of a fruitful and interesting lifestyle.

NEGATIVE CHARACTERISTICS

An unrealistic attitude to life can make it difficult for the Horus to realise ambitions. Complications can arise through failure to accept problems or avoid danger. Many born in this sign have a stubborn attitude, sometimes amounting to pig-headedness. Conflict with those in authority or incompatibility in family life is often a problem for the Horus. Most endeavours are all or nothing for the Horus and few born in this cycle leave anything in reserve.

APPEARANCE

Like the wings of the falcon, the arms are one of the most notable features of the Horus. They are long and graceful and the Horus tends to use them expressively in conversation, making wide and exaggerated gesticulations. Unless it is essential for those born in this cycle to dress up for an occasion most are content to wear whatever is at hand. When they do dress up, however, an unusual and individual style of dress is common amongst those born in this sign.

HEALTH

One problem that many a Horus shares is insomnia. Few born in this cycle sleep deeply or for long, and restless nights are common for this sign. This is especially true if the Horus is engaged in a particularly absorbing enterprise. Sometimes stress and long periods of activity can lead to headaches or migraines. For the Horus who has suffered a setback, there is a marked tendency toward melancholia or even depression.

WORDS OF ADVICE

Exceptionally creative, the Horus's ideas are often unconventional and original, attracting adverse criticism from those who are less imaginative. Few born in this cycle, though, will accept censure without a fight. Although others may hold unconventional views in private, the Horus says what they feel and expresses what they believe. This may lead to conflicts that could otherwise have been avoided. The Horus should learn to hold their tongue now and again and try a little harder to impress or even flatter those whose help they need. For the Horus, what happens today is far more important than what happened yesterday. The Horus should avoid burning the bridges they have crossed.

SUITABLE OCCUPATIONS

Many athletes, needing repeatedly to break the pain barrier or to push themselves beyond endurance, are born in this sign. Other ground-breaking Horus occupations often involve a high degree of personal risk. The Horus can make an extremely successful politician, easily handling the multifarious skills necessary for the role. They have excellent communicative ability, coupled with an attention-grabbing and persuasive form of expression. Few born in this sign fail to argue their point. For artistic pursuits, Horus is particularly creative sign. As managers or employers though, Horus is not always the best of signs. Those born in this cycle tend to lead far too readily from the front and fail to offer the support and encouragement others may need.

THE HORUS AT WORK

As a negotiator, the persistent Horus excels. Bargaining can be a long and arduous affair and the Horus is an able player at the waiting game. Those who believe that they are getting the better of any deal with the Horus are deluding themselves. The Horus will go through hell and high water to achieve their aims. Many born in this sign are self-made people, having a style all their own. However, headstrong emotions can send them forging ahead and others may find it difficult to keep pace. Many Horus people have an eccentric personality that workmates will either love or hate. The Horus will make a good ally but a formidable opponent.

THE HORUS WOMAN

Fashion sense does not come naturally for many Horus women. To those born in this sign, what they are doing is far more important than how they look. The Horus woman is prepared to dress well to suit an occasion or to conform at work. However, she looks her best in casual attire. A clean but scruffy look can suit her down to the ground, giving her an aura of relaxed confidence. Few Horus women feel comfortable if dressed to the nines.

The Horus woman can be the toughest of any sign. It is not that she lacks femininity; so determined is she to make her mark in the world that feminine poise is a low priority. She is a good socializer and is usually popular with other women – over whom she can exert much influence. Men may find her somewhat daunting as she controls the men in her life with little difficulty. Few women born in this cycle would suit the domineering male. The Horus picks out the man she wants and pursues him with determination.

THE HORUS MAN

Like his female counterpart, the Horus male is imaginative, witty and erudite. However, he is not every girl's idea of the perfect date. He can be marvellous company, full of anecdotes, jokes and fun. However, he has an unusual, sometimes eccentric manner that can be intimidating for some women. Moreover, he says exactly what he thinks, which may not always be what his partner wants to hear. Luckily, he prefers women with an unconventional attitude to life – few others can take the Horus man in their stride.

The Horus male is adventurous and is ever ready to lead. However, he seems unaware that others may have difficulty keeping pace. The Horus man is more of a gambler than the woman of this sign. He cannot resist the temptation of trying to make money the easy way. Concerning financial matters in general, the male Horus lacks the thrift of the female. He is often late with his bills and all too willing to obtain credit he cannot afford to repay. However, the Horus is luckier than many signs – his excesses sometimes pay off.

THE HORUS PARENT

The Horus is an affectionate and protective parent though not usually possessive. Their children are encouraged to be self-reliant and to mix freely with others. They like to be considered as friends to their children, and many offspring of the Horus enjoy their parent's company throughout their lives. Neither Horus mothers nor fathers suffer from the common problem of expecting too much of their young. They may have unrealistic ambitions for themselves but such harsh expectations are seldom inflicted on others.

THE HORUS CHILD

The Horus child is the most contrary of any sign. From an early age they are forever disagreeing with teachers or parents. It is no good merely telling a Horus child that something simply is – you will always be faced with an abrupt 'Why?' Many Horus children are hyperactive which, coupled with their natural inquisitiveness, can make them something of a handful. The questioning Horus is quick to learn, however, and providing their curiosity is accommodated they can be as entertaining as their adult counterparts.

Most children are untidy but the Horus especially so. On the positive side, they are generally concerned about the well-being of others, and few Horus children will be cruel or unkind. In fact they have a sympathetic attitude to others right from infancy, and are sometimes far too ready to offer assistance and help. When in trouble, children have a tendency to deny responsibility and accuse a friend or sibling. The Horus child, however, is usually willing to admit fault and may even take the blame on behalf of the friends.

THE HORUS FRIEND

The Horus is tremendous fun to have around. They share a marvellous, although unusual, sense of humour, live life to the full and can be the soul of any party. They have an abundance of energy, love being the centre of attention and have a great aptitude to think up novel and interesting schemes. However, the Horus can be somewhat draining – they never seem to stop. For some signs the Horus is best in small doses. Others who enjoy the unusual are often at their happiest in the company of the exciting Horus. But beware! The Horus also expects to share their problems. With most born in this sign, friendship is an all-or-nothing affair.

The Horus is quick to forgive and seldom holds a grudge – unless, that is, someone has deliberately done them harm. When the Horus has what they believe to be a justifiable grievance they are expert at exacting revenge. They can stir up trouble for their enemies by skilfully setting others at their throats, while all the time remaining apparently blameless.

The Horus may have much to say, but they often have little patience with mulling over old hurts or painfully analysing the past. Primarily, they live for today and tomorrow.

THE HORUS PARTNER

The Horus has no inclination to feign an interest in matters that fail to absorb them. If they are bored they will say so. This can sometimes lead to conflicting behaviour in the caring Horus. If impelled by circumstances to be involved in something in which they have no real interest, they consider it a tiresome, duty-bound responsibility. Consequently, they will carry out what is expected of them but make certain that everyone knows exactly how they feel. It is often advisable for a partner to exclude a Horus from anything in which they have no enthusiasm. The Horus will quite happily apply themselves to something else.

The Horus is a complainer, especially about the service in hotels, restaurants or stores. Indeed, on occasions, especially during journeys and vacations, the Horus can be a right pain with their grouching and moaning. It is usually a good idea for the Horus's partner to handle receptionists, waiters and other serving staff – it will certainly make life easier for everyone concerned.

Horus may not be the most romantic of partners for a date, but they desperately need love in their lives. Born in a particularly caring sign, they have a deeply sentimental streak and need and offer true affection. They may say exactly what they feel, they may be inclined to moan, but the Horus can fall madly in love and will make many a personal sacrifice to assure their partner's happiness. Those born in the sign of Horus may be individualists but they are certainly not loners.

HORUS AND OTHER SIGNS

AFFINITY SIGNS

OSIRIS: Both signs are particularly tolerant of one another. The Horus's shortcomings are similar to the Osiris's own, such as escaping wherever possible from tiresome responsibilities. Both hate to be tied down. With so many interests, the Horus seldom find themselves in conflict with the Osiris.

WADJET: Although the Wadjet and the Horus are opposites in many respects, their traits and attributes are complimentary. The Wadjet is patient and plans long and hard; the Horus can be impatient and impetuous. The Wadjet can restrain the Horus, while the Horus can bring more spontaneity to the Wadjets's life.

THE SPHINX: The Horus and the Sphinx often mix well. The Sphinx has many ideas that they lack the courage to try. The Horus is quite prepared to implement the Sphinx's schemes. These signs often make ideal partners in marriage.

PROBLEM SIGNS

THE PHOENIX: Potentially the most problematic sign for the Horus is the Phoenix. The Phoenix can recover well from failures but the Horus finds it hard. Both signs are adventurous but when the Phoenix burned it rose again. The two signs get on great to begin with but should problems occur the Phoenix cannot understand the Horus's inability to cope.

SEKHMET: The energetic Sekhmet and the stubborn Horus will often argue and bicker even when they see eye-to-eye.

SHU: The serenity of life style the Shu needs is unlikely to be found in close proximity to the Horus.

OTHER SIGNS

THOTH: Although the Thoth can make a good acquaintance, they do not necessarily make ideal partners for the Horus. The Thoth lacks the romantic affection that the Horus needs.

AMUN: The Horus is a particularly affectionate sign, and the Amun tends to distrust open displays of affection. The Amun, however, can sometimes provide an emotional balance for the Horus.

HATHOR: Horus and Hathor both allow their imaginations a free reign. Consequently, the two signs get on well but may behave irresponsibly when together.

ANUBIS: The Anubis and the Horus have few problems socially, although the Horus is seldom prepared to make the sort of long-term commitments Anubis expects.

HORUS: Together, those born in this sign tend to behave in a completely impractical manner and financial considerations are usually ignored. In social circumstances, however, they are usually fascinated by each other's attitude to life and they are ever ready to enjoy each other's company.

ISIS: As both Horus and Isis commit themselves so completely to a chosen pursuit, these two signs work well together if they share a similar heart-felt interest. If their interests lie in different directions, however, they are unlikely to have the time to spare for one another.

FATE AND FORTUNE

Over the course of the year the Horus can expect the following influences to affect their lives during the separate Egyptian months:

THOTH 29 AUGUST – 27 SEPTEMBER:

Thoth is the message-bearer for the Horus. During this month the Horus can expect favourable news.

HORUS 28 SEPTEMBER – 27 OCTOBER:

During their own month the Horus can be especially reckless. They should think long and deeply about any change of direction they may be considering. If an enterprise has been long established, however, a favourable turn of events is likely – provided that the Horus lets things be as they are.

WADJET 28 OCTOBER – 26 NOVEMBER:

The quick-fire serpent brings the Horus a period of much success in social and leisure activities. Sporting events are particularly favoured at this time. Indeed, games of any kind can be enjoyed to the full, often with remarkable success. A lucky month for ventures involving risk.

SEKHMET 27 NOVEMBER – 26 DECEMBER :

Anything concerning group activities, either social or business in nature, is well placed for the Horus. Any Horus who takes the initiative at this time of the year is likely to find themselves in a profitable position. This may be the most romantic month of the year for those born in the sign of Horus.

THE SPHINX 27 DECEMBER – 25 JANUARY :

It is the Sphinx's guardian role that engages for the Horus during this month. Nearly everything the Horus tries to accomplish seems to be prevented and all that the Horus hopes for seems to be delayed.

SHU 26 JANUARY – 24 FEBRUARY:

During the month of Shu the Horus's plans may prove impractical. They may find themselves out of touch with everyday events and relationships or social events may suffer from the Horus's unrealistic expectations.

ISIS 25 FEBRUARY – 26 MARCH :

Isis is a sign of change for the Horus. The Horus may feel impelled to change job, social or even romantic attachments at this time. Exciting and promising opportunities are also on the cards. This is a particularly good time for the Horus considering a change of any kind.

OSIRIS 27 MARCH – 25 APRIL:

Osiris has a positive affect on the Horus. Many of their imaginative enterprises will come to fruition. New relationships or business links formed at this time may prove positive for the Horus. Love, romance and affairs of the heart are particularly well favoured during this month.

AMUN 26 APRIL – 25 MAY :

During this month the Horus is often at their most adventurous. Their fun-loving disposition is best directed toward leisure activities and many will find a vacation exhilarating. Any Horus on the look out for new romantic attachments may be pleasantly surprised during this cycle.

HATHOR 26 MAY – 24 JUNE :

The month of Hathor is when the Horus is likely to make errors of judgement. The headstrong Hathor and Horus influences combined can result in a lack of tact or restraint.

THE PHOENIX 25 JUNE – 24 JULY:

The resourceful Phoenix brings many new opportunities for the Horus. At no other time of the year is the Horus so ready to succeed, especially in commercial ventures.

ANUBIS 25 JULY – 28 AUGUST:

This is one of the worst months for the Horus to make any important decisions or major changes in lifestyle. It is best to wait for the cycle of Anubis to be over before doing anything likely to cause long-term effects.

HORUS CORRESPONDENCES

STONE   CITRINE
TREE   ACACIA
FOOD   SUNFLOWER SEEDS
HERB   ROSEMARY
FLOWER   CARNATION

COLOUR   YELLOW GOLD
LUCKY NUMBER   6
INCENSE   FRANKINCENSE
ANIMAL   FALCON
SYMBOL

FAMOUS HORUSES

Scott Bakula, Neve Campbell, Aleister Crowley, Matt Damon,
Eminem, Hugh Jackman, Bela Lugosi, Gwyneth Paltrow, Jacquin
Phoenix, Julia Roberts, Alicia Silverstone, Kate Winslet.

HORUS WORKING

Oh Horus, great Heru
Who is Lord of the Sky
I call upon thee
Protect me from all ills that approach from the east.
O Horus, Dweller in the Shrine
Protect me from all ills that approach from the south.
Heru, Pillar of Isis.

Protect me from all ills that approach from the west.
Great God of Two Fold strength,
Protect me from all ills that approach from the north.
O Horus, Beauteous Face of Heaven
Remain at all times about me.
O Heru, Pa-neb-tawy.
Lord of the Two Lands
When I cannot hear, lead me.
Charioteer of the Celestial Sphere
When I cannot see, show me the way
Heru, Bringer of Light, Banisher of Darkness
Let me recognize and seize the opportunities that
  I am granted.

O Horus, Helmsman of the Divine Barge
Let thy hand work through me.
Guide me to my path of destiny.
Grant me now thy power.
O Heru, Pa-neb-tawy.

CHAPTER 3

· WADJET ·

28 OCTOBER–26 NOVEMBER

It is through the will of the great serpent goddess that all kings shall rule.

From the Pyramid Texts.

Wadjet, known also as Uatchat, was the royal cobra goddess of Ancient Egypt, who was supposed to have created the papyrus swamps of the Delta. As a deity of kingship, her image adorned the front of pharaoh's crown, when it was called the Uraeus. Depicted as a cobra poised to strike, Wadjet was a symbol of knowledge and those born in this sign often exude an aura of wisdom. Wadjet people have logical and calculating minds, formulating plans and waiting patiently for the precise moment to act. Although they enjoy the virtue of patience, they live constantly in a state of readiness. Like the snake, they strike instantly when the time is right. Wadjets are dedicated and conscientious workers. They are eager to learn and quick to find practical applications for their knowledge. So often it is the Wadjet who is called upon to deal with the problems others have failed to solve.

Wadjets are prepared to work long and hard to achieve their objectives. They are highly ambitious, seldom deterred by adversity and almost oblivious to hostile opinion. Although Wadjets share a pragmatic and materialistic attitude to life, they approach nothing in a dull or tedious fashion. Indeed, most Wadjets ooze enthusiasm for their chosen subjects. They may be given to high-spirited and frivolous behaviour in their spare time, but during working hours they are serious and determined. Wadjets are realists, directing their energy toward their endeavours with logic and common sense, rather than – what they would consider – lofty intuition.

Wadjets exercise enviable patience concerning most endeavours and accurately judge the correct moment to act. They also have the capacity to grasp the root of a problem, possessing shrewd insight into the real cause of difficulties they may face. In any enterprise the Wadjet will weigh up its potential long and hard before making decisions. Wadjets are forthright and astute, they have inquiring and probing minds and are remarkably self-disciplined.

POSITIVE CHARACTERISTICS

Wadjets have a serious outlook on life, coupled with a strong sense of responsibility. Their ambition is supported by a shrewd intellect and the ability to devote themselves exclusively to an enterprise. Observant and inquisitive, the Wadjet is quick to learn. They are especially loyal to their friends and take family values seriously. Mental energy is a marked feature of those born in this sign, together with a direct and decisive manner. Many Wadjets show considerable initiative in the handling of financial affairs.

NEGATIVE CHARACTERISTICS

A cynical temperament may restrict social activities. Often too ready to disregard the opinions of their acquaintances, arrogance is sometimes a Wadjet fault. Occasionally Wadjets share a less than sympathetic attitude to others. Wadjets also have a tendency to take themselves much too seriously at times. The Wadjet is economically minded and may be over-thrifty, even miserly.

APPEARANCE
Like the head of a swaying cobra, Wadjets will use their hands as a prominent means of expression. If they disagree, they will slice their hands through the air as if to cut the conversation dead and when they have had enough they will thrust out their palms to call for silence. Some snakes are said to mesmerize their prey. Many Wadjets have melodic voices possessing an almost hypnotic quality.

HEALTH
The Wadjet is especially susceptible to coughs and colds. If a flu virus is going around the Wadjet is sure to catch it. Cold, damp weather also plays havoc with those born in this sign. They thrive in the hottest of climates, but if it is chilly or wet the Wadjet is likely to suffer. Rheumatism, arthritis and similar complaints may be a problem for Wadjets, especially in later years.

WORDS OF ADVICE
Wadjets can be far too cynical at times, refusing to believe anything that has not been proved beyond reasonable doubt. They are

unlikely to take anything at face value or on someone else's word. Wadjets should try to have a little more faith in human nature. This may not be a perfect world but others are generally more honest than the Wadjet is prepared to give credit. Another Wadjet trait is the need to know the detailed affairs of those around them. Sometimes Wadjets are just too inquisitive for their own good. Few Wadjets will reveal their own motivations, feelings and intentions, however. Those born in this sign would make excellent poker players if they were inclined to gamble. To Wadjets, however, anything based chiefly upon luck is strictly a mug's game. The Wadjet should learn to take the occasional risk.

SUITABLE OCCUPATIONS
Wadjets make good entrepreneurs, managers or supervisors. They watch and listen carefully before arriving at conclusions, and then only after every angle has been considered. Accordingly, they make solid judgements and usually take sound commercial decisions. Furthermore, they are quick to assert authority in a firm, decisive manner. Occupations involving intricate, detailed or complex calculations are ideal for Wadjets. They work well with figures and excel in financial careers. Architects, designers and engineers also include many successful Wadjets. Their keen eye for detail also suits

the Wadjet for work involving proofreading, editing or copywriting. Wadjets are also suited to academic and teaching occupations and anything involving investigation or research.

THE WADJET AT WORK

Wadjets apply themselves with remarkable dedication. They have the enviable ability to concentrate fully on whatever they are doing. Employers can always rely on the Wadjet to do their job to the best of their ability. Snakes are solitary hunters and the same goes for many born in the Wadjet sign. They sometimes find it difficult to socialise with those with whom they work. Indeed, they may keep their work colleagues quite separate from their social lives.

THE WADJET WOMAN

Whatever the Wadjet woman puts her mind to she carries out in a responsible, determined and dedicated manner. She makes an ideal career woman but will seldom return to work once she has started a family. The Wadjet will devote herself exclusively to whatever she is doing. She can be an accomplished career woman and a devoted home-maker, but is unlikely to mix the two.

The Wadjet is a creature of thrift and economy. This is particularly true of the Wadjet woman. Whether or not she is a follower of fashion will depend very much on her chosen lifestyle. She is a smart dresser and takes pride in her appearance but has no intention of laying out good money to buy trendy clothes just for the sake of it. If her work necessitates a fashionable image, however, she will go to considerable lengths to make certain she is second to none. The Wadjet hostess, actress or model, for instance, will ensure she is wearing the very best and latest style. Indeed, Wadjets make some of the most successful women whose life is spent in the public eye or before the camera.

THE WADJET MAN

The Wadjet is a sociable man but refuses to involve himself in irrelevant small talk. He is sparing with his affections; others usually need to share his sentiments before he is prepared to commit himself to friendship. With his friends and loved ones the Wadjet is a mine of fascinating information. Not only will he know his pet subject inside out, he will air his opinions in the most engaging manner.

Like his female counterpart, the Wadjet man is keen on physical fitness. He may be a regular visitor to the gym, swimming baths or squash court but he is unlikely to be an ardent supporter or spectator. The Wadjet man has little enthusiasm for sporting events in which he has no personal stake. Many Wadjet men are more concerned with business affairs than leisure-time activities. The Wadjet man is a shrewd investor, well versed in the unwritten rules of the business world.

THE WADJET PARENT

Wadjets make responsible parents, devoting much time and effort to secure their children's future. They are exceptionally keen to see their children do well at school or in college. The child of a Wadjet parent is often an academic achiever. They enjoy considerable parental support and encouragement from an early age. Both Wadjet mothers and fathers are happy to teach their infants to read and write, while older children will benefit by the Wadjet's help with their homework. Wadjet parents spare no expense in stocking the home with books, learning aids and educational toys. They are prepared to spend their hard-earned money to ensure that their children get the very best start in life.

THE WADJET CHILD

Wadjets are studious children. They often devote more time to learning than they do to play. Indeed, they may need encouragement to mix with other children. Many Wadjet children actually prefer adult company. They mature early and are capable of standing their ground in most situations. Keen observation and intelligence combined with extraordinary intuition often results in 'an old head on young shoulders'. Wadjet children are constantly questioning the world about them, not satisfied until they have discovered the answer for everything that grabs their attention.

Unlike many young people, the Wadjet child is particularly good with finances. Pocket money is unlikely to be blown at the first opportunity on chocolates and candy but saved toward something more important such as holidays or Christmas presents. Like their adult counterparts, the Wadjet child is seldom wasteful and has a thrifty attitude toward life in general.

THE WADJET FRIEND

Although the Wadjet is a sign of confidence, many born in this cycle are wary of casual acquaintances. The Wadjet is cautious by nature and others may need to prove themselves worthy of their trust.

Wadjets expect much in return for their friendship. They expect to share and share alike with their friends and hate to feel excluded from any area of their lives. Friendships are usually all-or-nothing affairs for the Wadjet.

Although Wadjets are dedicated workers they also know how to have a good time. They will often devote themselves as much to entertainment as they do to work – an evening out is expected to be a fun-filled excursion. During social occasions, the one thing the Wadjet just cannot abide is someone talking shop. Those who continue an office conversation or bring up the subject of work are likely to find themselves immediately cut short by an irate Wadjet. Although they will readily enjoy themselves, Wadjets do not seek to be the centre of attention. The Wadjet may be self-assured but they are also self-conscious. Few Wadjets are prepared to make a fool of themselves on the dance floor or to get drunk and lose control.

THE WADJET PARTNER

Wadjets are seldom eager to show their feelings. They need to trust someone completely before sharing their true emotions. Consequently, the Wadjet partner may need to make all the first moves. Although witty in conversation, Wadjets are frequently shy with the opposite sex, finding it difficult to initiate a conversation with someone they find attractive. As women are not usually expected to make the first move, this is less of a problem for the Wadjet female. For the Wadjet male, however, it can sometimes hinder his love life. So often a girl will fail to realize that the Wadjet man is actually interested in her.

Wadjets are sensitive and committed lovers but break-ups are particularly difficult for them to handle. They hate the thought that they may have given so much of themselves only to be rejected. On the outside they seem to cope, but inside they may be devastated. A failed relationship can create an especially cynical Wadjet. Few Wadjets continue to chase or seek the attentions of an ex-partner – they have too much pride. The chief problem is for their next relationship. They may be suspicious of the true intentions of their future partner or restrained in the commitments they themselves are prepared to make. It can be some time before the Wadjet has recovered sufficiently to again abandon their emotional inhibitions.

WADJET AND OTHER SIGNS

AFFINITY SIGNS

AMUN: Wadjet is a sign of wisdom and those born in this cycle are particularly creative concerning practical endeavours. The Amun is a materialist and so the two signs compliment one another. Both signs lead similar social lives and close friendships and attachments are common.

HORUS: Although the Wadjet and the Horus are opposites in many respects, their traits and attributes are complimentary. The Wadjet is patient and plans long and hard; the Horus can be impatient and impetuous. The Wadjet can restrain the Horus, while the Horus can bring more spontaneity to the Wadjets's life.

THE SHPINX: The wise Wadjet and the cunning Sphinx usually share a common outlook on life and enjoy many of the same interests. Mutual respect, affection and compatibility are often found between these two signs.

ISIS: The Wadjet love of learning is much respected by the Isis. The Wadjet finds the Isis's unique insight equally fascinating. The two signs work well together and marriages are often successful.

PROBLEM SIGNS

THOTH: The Wadjet is generally a sign where the Thoth finds greatest difficulty. Wadjets enjoy taking charge too much for Thoth's liking.

THE PHOENIX: Those born in the sign of the Phoenix find it difficult to cope with the leadership qualities of the Wadjet. Wadjets sometimes find Phoenixes too inconsistent in their behaviour.

WADJET: As many Wadjets are somewhat reserved by nature, and unwilling to reveal their inner feelings, two Wadjets together tend to be overcautious in their attitudes to one another.

OTHER SIGNS

OSIRIS: The Wadjet and the Osiris mix well enough, although close relationships are rare. Wadjets are too pragmatic and take life too seriously for the Osiris. Many Wadjets consider the Osiris to be irresponsible.

HATHOR: The Hathor finds the learned Wadjet of considerable interest. They may, however, distrust the Wadjet's cool, laid-back approach to life.

SHU: Shus and Wadjets share little in common. However, this can sometimes lead to successful marriages. There is little for them to argue or disagree about.

ANUBIS: The Anubis likes to know precisely where they stand with others and most find the Wadjet difficult to fathom.

SEKHMET: Many Wadjets feel that Sekhmets reveal too much about themselves and some may regard this as a weakness. Sekhmets, for their part, may consider that Wadjets lead a far too conventional lifestyle.

FATE AND FORTUNE

Over the course of the year the Wadjet can expect the following influences to affect their lives during the separate Egyptian months:

THOTH 29 AUGUST – 27 SEPTEMBER:

The month of Thoth can be full of surprises for the Wadjet. This is also an excellent time for a vacation.

HORUS 28 SEPTEMBER – 27 OCTOBER:

Horus acts as the message bearer for the Wadjet. Wadjets can expect favourable news during this month.

WADJET 28 OCTOBER – 26 NOVEMBER:

Wadjets work remarkably well during their own month. For Wadjets involved in academic pursuits, this is a month of much reward. Wadjets in business also fare particularly well during this cycle. In domestic affairs, positive news concerning financial affairs can be expected.

SEKHMET 27 NOVEMBER – 26 DECEMBER:

There could be conflicts of interest during this month. Particularly in relationships, the Wadjet should avoid disputes. The working Wadjet should also be careful of disagreements in the factory or office – things may not work out the way they intended.

THE SPHINX 27 DECEMBER – 25 JANUARY:

The Wadjet has little difficulty solving the Sphinx's eternal riddle. A long-standing enterprise may come to fruition. This is a time especially favourable for new relationships, romance and love. It is also a lucky month for anything connected with chance.

SHU 26 JANUARY – 24 FEBRUARY:

Shu is light and air while the serpent lives its life on the ground. The two signs accordingly have little influence upon one another. This can be a time of inactivity, even boredom, for the Wadjet.

ISIS 25 FEBRUARY – 26 MARCH:

The month of Isis can bring a Wadjet plan to fruition. It is also the time of year when new opportunities arise. It is an especially good period for a change of job or location should either be sought.

OSIRIS 27 MARCH – 25 APRIL:

Osiris is a positive sign for the Wadjet. This is a favourable month for relationships to flourish. Success is especially likely for the Wadjet on the lookout for a new partner.

AMUN 26 APRIL – 25 MAY:

Wadjets are inquisitive and like to know exactly what is going on around them. The multifarious Amun can cloud the Wadjet's vision – there may be too much happening for Wadjets to see in all directions. They should avoid being suspicious of situations of which they are not fully informed.

HATHOR 26 MAY – 24 JUNE:

The Wadjet is a creature of the earth and so is Hathor. The two signs work well together, and the Wadjet will find that others will see things their way. This is a particularly favourable month for sport and leisure activities. Any Wadjet involved in competition is likely to be rewarded with much success.

THE PHOENIX 25 JUNE – 24 JULY:

The usual success of the Wadjet's quick-fire response can be upset during the month of the Phoenix. In legend the Phoenix burned to ashes and so opportunities can go up in smoke for a Wadjet during this cycle.

ANUBIS 25 JULY – 28 AUGUST:

In the month of Anubis financial matters and business affairs are well placed. This is also a romantic month for the Wadjet.

WADJET CORRESPONDENCES

STONE   AMETHYST
TREE   ASH
FOOD   LEMON
HERB   MUSTARD
FLOWER   HYACINTH

COLOUR   LILAC
LUCKY NUMBER   10
INCENSE   ROSE
ANIMAL   SERPENT
SYMBOL

FAMOUS WADJETS

Jennifer Aniston, Björk, Lisa Bonet, Petula Clark, Leonardo Di Caprio, Callista Flockhart, Ethan Hawke, Winona Rider, David Schwimmer.

WADJET WORKING

Oh Wadjet,
Great Lady of Heaven
I call upon thee.
Protect me from all ills that approach from the east.
O Uatchet, Solar and Eternal Serpent
Protect me from all ills that approach from the south.
O Wadjet, Dweller in the Stone of Kadesh
Protect me from all ills that approach from the west.

Great Goddess, Mother of Nefertum the Beautiful
Protect me from all ills that approach from the north.
O Wadjet, Opener of the Way
Remain at all times about me.
Ateh Am-enti, Ateh Per-menat.
When I cannot hear, lead me.

O Wadjet, Mistress of all the Gods
When I cannot see, show me the way.
O Uatchet, who came forth from Horus
To adorn the head of Ra
Let me recognize and seize the opportunities that
   I am granted.
O Wadjet, Power of the Uraeus
Let thy hand work through me.
Guide me to my path of destiny.
Grant me now thy power.
Ateh Am-enti, Ateh Per-menat.

CHAPTER 4

· SEKHMET ·

27 NOVEMBER–26 DECEMBER

O mighty one, great of magic, wise and powerful daughter of Re.

An eighteenth-dynasty inscription of the temple of Mut.

The lioness-headed Sekhmet was both a war and desert goddess. She was also the mistress of fire and known as the 'eye of Ra', exemplifying the intense heat of the sun. The fire-breathing Sekhmet was perhaps the most feared of all Egyptian gods, yet she was also seen as a deity of mystical power, and paradoxically, a goddess of healing. Sekhmet's priests were also physicians. Others may feel vulnerable in the presence of those born in this sign.

Nevertheless, many seek their guidance and leadership. Sekhmets, however, are reluctant leaders, usually preferring to go it alone. Blessed with an abundance of mental energy, they are capable of handling most tasks that befall them. Natural creatures of fire, Sekhmets have the enviable capacity not to get burned and usually land firmly on their feet.

Sekhmets possess intellectual vitality, mental dexterity and a lively imagination. The Sekhmet is one of the most eloquent of signs and many Sekhmets can argue an opponent blue in the face. Those born in this cycle have endless optimism for their chosen pursuits. Forever formulating plans and new ideas, Sekhmets can sometimes be tiring, even draining, on friends and acquaintances. Not only are Sekhmets blessed with boundless faith and optimism, they are also endowed with vision and foresight. They have a deep sense of intuition and seem to know precisely what others are thinking and planning. An alert mind enables Sekhmets to determine the full potential of opportunities and make quick decisions. Sekhmets are highly active and many born in this sign excel in sport and games.

Sekhmets work remarkably well in short, sharp bursts. They apply themselves with speed and determination to whatever they are doing. They have a multiplicity of talents, both creative and practical. With an astute memory and inquiring mind, those born in this sign are especially clever at arguing a point. They can skilfully sidetrack an opponent and have them tied up with their own words. Many Sekhmets are highly intelligent and able to grasp the most complex of problems. They excel at solving conundrums or riddles of any kind. Sekhmets are exceptionally optimistic and refuse to concede defeat under any circumstances. They make quick decisions and act decisively.

POSITIVE CHARACTERISTICS

An energetic personality guarantees the Sekhmet success in most undertakings. Extremely versatile, they can turn their hands to many endeavours. Mentally agile and quick to learn, the majority of those born in this sign are observant and possess a remarkably good memory. They have artistic talents, especially concerning writing and music, and express themselves in a popular, dramatic fashion. With an exceptional ability to cope in times of difficulty, Sekhmets are optimistic and enthusiastic about whatever they are doing.

NEGATIVE CHARACTERISTICS

Sekhmets are unwilling to change opinions, even when proved wrong. They are impatient, jump to conclusions far too quickly and are apt to make errors of judgement based on hasty decisions or first impressions. Many born in this sign have a quarrelsome temperament, often disagreeing for the sheer sake of it. Impulsiveness sometimes stems from this love of action and there is a tendency for Sekhmets to rush headlong into ventures much too readily.

APPEARANCE

Sekhmets are energetic and restless, finding it difficult to sit quietly for any length of time. They need to be constantly occupied, many being slim or even skinny as a consequence of the nervous energy they expend. Many born in this sign have expressive faces with a rigidly defined bone structure and penetrating eyes.

HEALTH

Sekhmets are remarkably resilient to viral infections, usually immune to the coughs and colds to which others annually succumb. They seldom get headaches, stomach bugs or any such common complaints. When the Sekhmet does fall ill – which is rarely – it is generally with something exotic or unusual. The only drawback to

Sekhmet's robust constitution is their need for sleep. Deprived of their eight or more hours, Sekhmets will virtually cease to function. At best, the tired Sekhmet will be irritable, grumpy and unable to concentrate.

WORDS OF ADVICE

In excess, Sekhmet's positive attributes become negative traits. Their optimistic streak is a considerable drawback if something is an obvious failure. Their blanket refusal to concede defeat will sometimes tie Sekhmet to a doomed endeavour, preventing them from applying themselves to anything fresh. Their displays of boundless enthusiasm can also be misleading to others. Acquaintances may be captivated by a Sekhmet's idea, only to discover that Sekhmet's interest was only superficial. Sekhmets should try to moderate their behaviour. It is not that they are deceitful – they simply have tunnel vision.

SUITABLE OCCUPATIONS

Sekhmets are suited for occupations involving quick reactions or calculations. They also excel in work that necessitates close customer contact such as sales. They have a lively personality with a friendly and enthusiastic countenance. Many lecturers and teachers are born in this sign, as are writers and broadcasters. Journalism and other investigative work also have strong appeal to Sekhmets. Their mental dexterity, often coupled with a devotion to physical fitness, means that many professional athletes and successful sportspeople are born in this sign.

THE SEKHMET AT WORK

Sekhmets value their freedom above all else. They hate being restricted or compromised in any situation. For this reason they are best suited to occupations which allow them freedom of movement and the scope to make decisions and handle matters in their own fashion. Sekhmets aim to reach the very pinnacle of whatever profession they choose. Even when not in a position of power they need the authority to use their own initiative. They are generally popular with colleagues, although they may sometimes disturb those with whom they work closely. Sekhmets have a tendency to adopt a loud or flamboyant working style.

THE SEKHMET WOMAN

Sekhmet woman has an aura of self-confidence and a glowing personality. Unlike Sekhmet men who sometimes keep their fiery temperament hidden beneath a cool exterior, the Sekhmet woman will often display her vitality to full advantage. She is every bit a lady, however, even though she may be something of a tomboy in her youth. Many women born in this sign are keen on physical fitness and most can hold their ground in male company.

Sekhmet is not the tidiest of women, quite content to slop around her home in jeans, an old sweater or a tracksuit. It is a different matter when she is at work or attending a special engagement – then she will dress to impress. The Sekhmet career woman will appear neat and efficient, whereas the Sekhmet woman at a social occasion will dress in a particularly feminine style. She will always look the part in whatever she is doing. A great lover of animals, Sekhmet woman is likely to own many pets. Even if her circumstances only permit her a single cat or dog, it will be treated as one of the family.

THE SEKHMET MAN
The male of this sign is often a born performer. Not only is he an excellent entertainer, at ease in most circumstances, he will adapt his style and humour to suit the occasion. The Sekhmet man loves to surround his life with excitement, even mystery. Unlike some signs who may find it necessary to create an enigmatic aura to hide a lack

of self-confidence, Sekhmet just loves to fascinate those around him. Sekhmet man is a boy at heart. Always eager to be the centre of attention, he is the life and soul of any party.

Most Sekhmet men are attracted to dominant women. Indeed, an assertive partner is often essential for the Sekhmet man. He is one of the laziest and untidy of men when it comes to household or domestic matters, needing someone who is prepared to handle this side of his life. If he does marry a more subservient woman the home environment is likely to end up a right old mess.

THE SEKHMET PARENT

Sekhmets encourage their children to do well, although they will seldom push them too hard. They usually manage to inspire their children through sheer enthusiasm. Sekhmets have the marvellous ability to make life interesting, and learning can be a fascinating and exciting experience for children of a Sekhmet mother or father. Both are always ready to take time from whatever they are doing – no matter how important – to help and advise their young. Sekhmets run a happy but not a particularly tidy home. They are ready to go to any lengths to prepare their children for working life, but neatness and orderly habits are something their offspring will need to learn elsewhere.

THE SEKHMET CHILD

Sekhmets are some of the most hyperactive children. They demand much attention and need many outlets for their energy. They mix well with others, young and old alike, but have a tendency to monopolize everyone in their vicinity. They may be gifted artistically, academically or technically but the ability to apply themselves to school or college work is often lacking. They are just too easily distracted. Their intelligence and capacity to rapidly assimilate information provides many born in this sign with the potential to be top of the class – if only they concentrate a little more.

The young Sekhmet may lack concentration in school, gazing through the classroom window at something more exciting outside. When they apply themselves, however, they are immensely creative achievers. Although they may become good sportspeople in their mid teens, sporting events are not high on the list of the younger Sekhmet's priorities. The Sekhmet child prefers to perform alone rather than as part of an organized group or team.

THE SEKHMET FRIEND

Sekhmets share a marvellous sense of humour. They always have the right joke or pertinent remark for any occasion. They are hospitable and friendly, although they often share an unusual, sometimes zany sense of humour. Sekhmets need to be constantly occupied and their friends will seldom be bored in their company.

Sekhmets are not particularly keen on the more conservative forms of entertainment. Sitting quietly at the theatre or cinema, or just relaxing in front of the television, is unlikely to appeal to many born in the Sekhmet sign. They prefer to be actively entertained, if not personally involved. Sekhmets intend to live life to the full and usually expect others to do likewise. If a friend prefers a more serene lifestyle, they are unlikely to get much peace with the Sekhmet around. Sekhmets like to keep in touch with distant friends, but their circle of acquaintances is often so large that it may be some time before they finally get around to contacting each in turn.

One annoying habit that is almost Sekhmet's trademark is the tendency for them to take far too long to get ready to go out. 'I'll just be a minute,' Sekhmet will promise, and an hour later you're still waiting. Regardless of excuses, Sekhmet is hopeless when it comes to estimating how long anything is going to take.

THE SEKHMET PARTNER

Few Sekhmets will happily spend time alone. They need company to be truly content. Consequently, Sekhmets will seldom be without a partner for long. Many marry early and those who don't will spend as much time as possible with their partner. They are not domineering or possessive, they just need someone around to give them encouragement and much-needed companionship.

Both men and women of this sign are passionate and uninhibited lovers and give themselves fully to romance. A love of variety and adventure makes Sekhmets exciting and stimulating partners. Although both Sekhmet men and women are often excessive in their chosen pursuits, they are usually careful with their money. A girl expecting endless gifts or an expensive night out from her Sekhmet man is in for disappointment. A man hoping to go Dutch and share the cost of a date with his Sekhmet girl is also in for a shock. Sekhmets are not averse to luxury: they just refuse to spend their hard-earned money in an extravagant or profitless way.

SEKHMET AND OTHER SIGNS

AFFINITY SIGNS

AMUN: The industrious and optimistic Sekhmet is admired by the Amun. Both signs share the ability to consistently devote themselves to a single goal or objective.

THE SPHINX: The Sphinx is often cool and relaxed in most situations. The hyperactive Sekhmet seldom disturbs the Sphinx, while the Sphinx's cunning and lively intelligence is much appreciated by the Sekhmet. These two signs compliment each other nicely, although it may seem to others that Sphinxes and Sekhmets are worlds apart.

SEKHMET: Most Sekhmets enjoy the company of others like themselves. Although they will often be messy or untidy together, they make excellent close friends and partners, sharing a love of excitement and adventure.

ISIS: Isis can take the energetic Sekhmet in their stride. The Sekhmet often needs a benevolent and controlling hand that the Isis is prepared to offer. Almost every attribute lacking in each sign is compensated by the attributes of the other, and some of the most successful marriages are formed between the Isis and the Sekhmet.

PROBLEM SIGNS

HORUS: The energetic Sekhmet and the stubborn Horus will often argue and bicker even when they see eye-to-eye.

ANUBIS: Sekhmets and Anubis people share similar creativity. However, the headstrong Anubis can often clash with the fiery temperament of the Sekhmet. Neither is prepared to give way to the other.

SHU: Sekhmet's energetic mentality is fascinating, though exhausting, to the peace-loving Shu.

OTHER SIGNS

OSIRIS: Sekhmets like to commit themselves to long-term relationships. The Osiris is quickly irritated by anything that becomes routine or lacks variety.

THE PHOENIX: Both Sekhmet and the Phoenix are signs of extreme optimism, and the two get on like a house on fire – after all, they are both creatures of fire. Unfortunately, together they tend to lack restraint: the Phoenix and the Sekhmet can find themselves in adverse situations that are difficult to remedy.

THOTH: The Thoth admires the Sekhmet's optimism and determinism, although the Thoth may become frustrated by the Sekhmet's abrupt changes of plans and their failure to see the obvious.

HATHOR: Relationships between Hathors and Sekhmets are particularly volatile. They may adore one another, sharing a love of adventure, travel and excitement. When together, however, both can find their emotions too readily stimulated and arguments may ensue. These signs often share a love/hate relationship.

WADJET: Many Wadjets feel that Sekhmets reveal too much about themselves, and some may regard this as a weakness. Sekhmets, for their part, may consider that Wadjets lead a far too conventional lifestyle.

FATE AND FORTUNE

Over the course of the year the Sekhmet can expect the following influences to affect their lives during the separate Egyptian months:

THOTH 29 AUGUST – 27 SEPTEMBER:

The month of Thoth is a time of much activity for Sekhmets, but they should be careful not to overwork. Sekhmets may become touchy or sensitive concerning the opinions of others. It is, however, an extremely favourable time for sport and other leisure activities.

HORUS 28 SEPTEMBER – 27 OCTOBER:

Anything concerning group activities, either social or business in nature, is well placed for the Sekhmet. Sekhmets who take the lead at this time of the year are likely to find themselves in a fortuitous or profitable situation.

WADJET 28 OCTOBER – 26 NOVEMBER:

Sekhmet and Wadjet are similar creatures of fire and, as such, there could be conflicts of interest during this month. Particularly concerning relationships, Sekhmet should be careful about involving themselves in disputes – they will probably end up the worst off.

SEKHMET 27 NOVEMBER – 26 DECEMBER:

During their own month many Sekhmets find excitement and adventure, particularly in romance and love. However, Sekhmet is an especially active creature and should take care not to work too hard during this period.

THE SPHINX 27 DECEMBER – 25 JANUARY:

The Sphinx is the message bearer for Sekhmet, and unusual news may arrive in the earlier days of this cycle. Sekhmet is still well placed for romance during the month of the Sphinx, while new acquaintances – particularly connected with financial matters – are very much on the cards.

SHU 26 JANUARY – 24 FEBRUARY:

Shu is swift and graceful while Sekhmet is strong and powerful. Sekhmet may accordingly overwhelm any subtle influence that the Shu month may bring. During this cycle Sekhmets should be particularly attentive to the smaller details of life, lest they overlook important, sometimes obvious possibilities.

ISIS 25 FEBRUARY – 26 MARCH:

The Isis month is a time of new possibilities, and anything the Sekhmet has been putting off should be considered at this time. Many Sekhmets find that most things tend to go right for them at this time of the year.

OSIRIS 27 MARCH – 25 APRIL:

Few Sekhmets will find the Osiris month a time of peace or tranquillity. Domestic circumstances may require much of Sekhmet's attention. If Sekhmets make certain to divide their time equally between work, rest and play this month should go by quite favourably.

AMUN 26 APRIL – 25 MAY:

At no other time of the year is Sekhmet more likely to lose patience than during the month of Amun. Problems in relationships with close friends or relatives may occur as a result of Sekhmet irritability.

HATHOR 26 MAY – 24 JUNE:

The month of the Hathor is a time when Sekhmets are exceptionally lucky. They should be careful, however, not to overplay their hand. If they know when to call it a day, the Hathor month can bring fulfilment in nearly every aspect of the Sekhmet's life.

THE PHOENIX 25 JUNE – 24 JULY:

Both the Phoenix and Sekhmet are fire signs in the extreme. During this month Sekhmet imagination will be at its most inventive. New projects are likely to succeed due to quick reactions. Romance is especially favoured, and new and exciting relationships are likely to be formed.

ANUBIS 25 JULY – 28 AUGUST:

Travel and change of work or location is favoured during the month of Anubis. If the Sekhmet intends to move house this can be a particularly good time to begin the process. Similarly, if they are considering a change of job they should profit by looking for new work at this time. If content to stay put, however, it is a favourable period for seeking promotion or expansion.

SEKHMET CORRESPONDENCES

STONE   TIGER'S-EYE
TREE   SANDALWOOD
FOOD   CINNAMON
HERB   PEPPER
FLOWER   POPPY

COLOUR   RED
LUCKY NUMBER   5
INCENSE   RED SANDALWOOD
ANIMAL   LIONESS
SYMBOL

FAMOUS SEKHMETS

Christina Aguilera, Dido, Samuel L. Jackson, Mary, Queen of Scots,
Jim Morrison, Michael Owen, Brad Pitt, Britney Spears.

SEKHMET WORKING

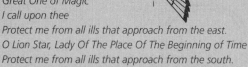

O Sekhmet,
Great One of Magic
I call upon thee
Protect me from all ills that approach from the east.
O Lion Star, Lady Of The Place Of The Beginning of Time
Protect me from all ills that approach from the south.
O Sekhmet, Lady Of The Many Faces

Protect me from all ills that approach from the west.
O Gold, Lady Of The Waters Of Life
Protect me from all ills that approach from the north.
O Sekhmet, Ruler Of The Chamber Of Flames

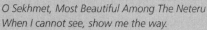

Remain at all times about me
Sekhet-Nes-ert, Sekhet Nes-Ert, Sekhet-Nes-Ert.
When I cannot hear, lead me.
O Sekhmet, Most Beautiful Among The Neteru
When I cannot see, show me the way.
O Sekhmet, Shining Of Countenance
Let me recognize and seize the opportunities that
*   I am granted.*
O Sekhmet, Adorable One

Let thy hand work through me.
Guide me to my path of destiny.
Grant me now thy power.
Sekhet-Nes-ert, Sekhet Nes-Ert, Sekhet-Nes-Ert.

CHAPTER 5

· **THE SPHINX** ·

27 DECEMBER-25 JANUARY

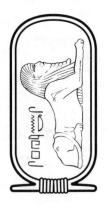

None can solve the riddle of the Sphinx, be he god or mortal man.

Diodurus Siculus, ancient Greek historian.

This is probably the most enigmatic of all the signs. In Egyptian mythology the Sphinx (whose original Egyptian name was 'Hu'), was not only a treasure guardian but also a shape shifter, able to change into the form of any other creature. Similarly, those born in the sign of the Sphinx share many characteristics with other signs. Sphinxes can modify and adapt their behaviour to suit their present company and current predicament. In Greek legend, the Sphinx set a riddle to be solved before its secrets would be revealed. Those born in this sign are forever challenging the world around them. They possess a mischievous quality that sometimes bewilders those about them, and few but the most perceptive will know the Sphinx's true intentions.

The Sphinx was also a sign of mystical power and another remarkable Sphinx trait is uncanny foresight. More often than not, circumstances will unfold just the way the Sphinx predicted. This unusual ability is due to a deep sense of intuition: an instinctive awareness that would make the Sphinx an excellent detective. They also have the capacity to grasp the root of a problem, possessing shrewd insight into the true cause of difficulties they encounter. Sphinxes are forthright and astute; they have inquiring and probing minds and are remarkably self-disciplined.

Sphinxes are always eager for new experiences and ready to rise to any challenge. However, they do not endeavour to fill their days with such excitement that they forget about the more practical matters of life. Sphinxes will keep a watchful eye on every detail of their ventures. They can create opportunities from very little and are one of the most enterprising of signs. They seldom, if ever, jump to conclusions and rarely allow prejudice to cloud their judgement. They have patience concerning most endeavours and accurately gauge the right moment to act.

POSITIVE CHARACTERISTICS

Outwardly the Sphinx is humorous, witty and fun-loving, but inwardly they maintain a serious, sharp-eyed attitude to life. They are ambitious with the capacity to exercise authority, while a strong will and conscientious attitude results in many Sphinxes holding positions of responsibility. Sphinxes are usually optimistic concerning their chosen ventures and a strong sense of intuition often brings them success. They have considerable powers of concentration, coupled with manifold technical and artistic skills. Those born in this cycle are also extremely self-disciplined, possessing the mental stamina to remain on top of most situations.

NEGATIVE CHARACTERISTICS

Opportunities are sometimes missed through too great an attachment to outdated ideas or methods. Sphinxes tend to make errors of judgement based on strongly held opinions. Others may consider Sphinxes to be arrogant or vain at times. They may also find Sphinx intuition disturbing. Sphinxes are often too inquisitive for their own good. In times of difficulty there is also a marked tendency for Sphinxes to blame others for problems of their own making.

APPEARANCE

The Sphinx has firm features and a confident and authoritative stature. They usually have a benevolent gaze and exude an aura of self-assuredness. They move with an air of certainty, they carry their heads high and walk with their backs straight. Few are quick or erratic; most being slow and deliberate movers.

HEALTH

The Sphinx is a sign of physical activity and so injuries and broken limbs are common for those born in this cycle. Few Sphinxes are worriers and so are seldom concerned about their own welfare. Many are inclined to ignore preventative medicine or disregard any tell-tale signs of illness. Repetitive strain injuries, or others ailments that are best tackled early, may be left unattended. This can lead to complications that might easily have been avoided.

WORDS OF ADVICE

Sphinxes can be far too cynical at times, refusing to believe anything they have not seen with their own eyes. They are unlikely to take anything at face value or on someone else's word. Sphinxes should try to have a little more faith in human nature. Sphinxes also feel impelled to know the detailed affairs of those around them and are sometimes too inquisitive for their own good. By contrast, few Sphinxes will reveal their own motivations or intentions. Sphinxes should learn to give and take a little more, particularly in business or professional matters.

SUITABLE OCCUPATIONS

Whether manual or white-collar workers, the Sphinx is generally most successful when self-employed. Sphinxes make especially good entrepreneurs, managers or supervisors. They watch and listen carefully before arriving at conclusions and only after every angle has been considered. Accordingly, they make solid judgements and usually take sound commercial decisions. Furthermore, they are quick to assert authority in a firm, decisive manner. Because of their multifarious attributes, Sphinxes are found in just about any occupation, and can easily change horses in mid-stream should the need arise.

THE SPHINX AT WORK

In business, success is assured providing colleagues are prepared to let the Sphinx do things their own way. Sphinxes make tough but fair employers, although they may drive their employees a little too hard. They are equally hard on themselves, however, and commit their many talents with remarkable dedication. They have the enviable ability to concentrate fully on whatever they are doing, and can always be trusted to do any job to the best of their ability. They share common traits with the Wadjet, finding it difficult to socialise with close business associates. Many Sphinxes keep their working lives quite separate from their social lives.

THE SPHINX WOMAN

The Sphinx woman is a great conversationalist and an eager listener. Many men are enchanted by her eloquent manner and flamboyant personality. She has an enigmatic demeanour that allows her to stand out from the crowd. The Sphinx woman enjoys much attention and so she may be the object of jealousy. The Sphinx will take a central role in social activities, and in business makes one of the most successful career women. She is always ready to give advice and is prepared to offer comfort to those in distress. She keeps her own problems very much to herself, however. Outwardly, she may seem unemotional and, unless angered, she will keep her true feelings very much to herself.

Most women born in the cycle of the Sphinx are neat and tidy, although they are more concerned with personal appearance than domestic order. The Sphinx woman usually spends so much time concentrating on her hair, clothes and make-up, that housework is often left unattended. The Sphinx woman is certain to be wearing the latest style, but nothing outrageous or unusual.

THE SPHINX MAN
The male of this sign is a born performer, an excellent entertainer and at ease in most company. He loves to surround his life with excitement and can adapt his character and humour to suit the occasion. The Sphinx will fascinate those around him and is always prepared to be the centre of attention. Not only are Sphinxes learned and knowledgeable on so many subjects, they will discuss anything in an enlightening and entertaining manner.

Sphinx men will divide their time equally between business affairs and leisure activities. They are, albeit, somewhat ruthless in commercial dealings. The Sphinx man expects his competitors and rivals to be as hardened as he. However, when all is said and done, the Sphinx is a social animal and loves to make everything as enjoyable as possible. Sphinx men are sparing with their deepest affections and expect others to share their sentiments before they are prepared to commit themselves to long-lasting friendships or relationships. To all those who share their life, Sphinxes are fascinating acquaintances.

THE SPHINX PARENT

Although caring, Sphinx parents are inclined to treat their family like an efficient business concern. Sphinx fathers have a tendency to act like firm but fair employers, while Sphinx mothers are especially concerned about their children's appearance. Both will ensure that their children are well looked after, but each has a tendency to concentrate too much on the child's physical welfare. To them, health, appearance, good manners and practical achievements are sometimes regarded to the exclusion of a child's emotional needs. Nevertheless, Sphinxes are benevolent and affectionate, merely wanting the very best for their young.

THE SPHINX CHILD

Right from infancy, the Sphinx child will be responsive to education and eager to learn. Sphinx children are inquisitive in the extreme, wanting to know the reason for everything. They work diligently at school and usually do well in class. There are seldom bad reports of the Sphinx child's academic achievements and most also do well in sport. Many children of this sign are born competitors.

The Sphinx child has a constructive attitude to life and few born in this cycle are likely to be rude, unkind or destructive in any way. They mix well with other children and are polite to adults, though many need constant attention and praise for their achievements. Their leadership qualities develop early and the little Sphinx will often insist on taking the lead with friends.

THE SPHINX FRIEND

Usually the Sphinx will read a situation perfectly. They often have tremendous insight into what is both appealing and popular and can captivate their friends with original and imaginative ideas. The Sphinx is not only a sign of creativity, it is also a sign of communication – many born in this cycle make the most entertaining hosts and companions.

Sphinxes have versatility of character and can adapt themselves to most company. Many are natural actors and will assume a personality tailor-made for a particular occasion. Innate performing skills are a usual Sphinx trait, and many born in this sign fit readily into whatever circumstances surround them. The Sphinx has a firm sense of loyalty, and close family ties need to be accepted by friends and lovers alike.

THE SPHINX PARTNER

The Sphinx is a sign of insight and most born in this cycle know precisely the right way to treat a prospective partner. They can readily adapt themselves to saying what others hope to hear, and will act to impress. There is nothing false about this remarkable Sphinx versatility. Sphinxes simply enjoy fitting in with others and with the spirit of an occasion.

Sphinxes have silver tongues, and Sphinx praise and flattery is hard to ignore. Romantics will find themselves captivated by the magnetic personality of the extroverted, self-assured Sphinx. They can adapt their interests and outlooks on life to suit their lover, and are often the most accommodating of partners. Sphinxes so hate discord in their domestic lives that they will go to tremendous lengths to avoid domestic squabbles or lover's tiffs. Unless an argument concerns something about which they feel deeply, Sphinxes much prefer to concede defeat for the sake of peace.

Sphinxes have a mysterious, enigmatic quality that others either love or fear. The Sphinx is usually so good at whatever they turn their minds to that they can be somewhat arrogant at times. This is seldom hollow vanity, rather an assured confidence which may be misconstrued. Like the enigmatic side of their nature, Sphinx assuredness is either distrusted or admired.

THE SPHINX AND OTHER SIGNS

AFFINITY SIGNS

AMUN: The Sphinx is the sign that the Amun often admires the most. Their ability to make something out of nothing, together with their keen financial instinct, are greatly respected by the Amun.

WADJET: The wise Wadjet and the cunning Sphinx usually share a common outlook on life and enjoy many of the same interests. Mutual respect, affection and compatibility are often found between these two signs.

SEKHMET: The Sphinx is cool and relaxed in most situations. The hyperactive Sekhmet seldom disturbs the Sphinx, while the Sphinx's cunning and lively intelligence is much appreciated by the Sekhmet. These two signs compliment each other nicely, although it may seem to others that Sphinxes and Sekhmets are worlds apart.

HORUS: The Horus and the Sphinx often mix well. The Sphinx has many ideas that they lack the courage to try. The Horus is quite prepared to implement the Sphinx's schemes. These signs often make ideal partners in marriage.

PROBLEM SIGNS

THOTH: The Sphinx is the sign that the Thoth finds hardest to fathom. Their ability to make something out of nothing, and their keen financial sense, are mysteries to the Thoth.

ANUBIS: Those born in the Sphinx and Anubis signs often experience a clash or interests and personality. Sometimes they may even distrust one another.

OSIRIS: The meticulous Sphinx can be most annoying to the Osiris. The two signs have markedly different temperaments and little in common.

THE SPHINX [27 December–25 January]   91

ISIS: Isis is a sign that can solve the Sphinx's eternal riddle. Isis intuition gives them the ability to fathom the motives of those born in the cycle of the Sphinx. The Sphinx may find this acutely unnerving.

OTHER SIGNS

THE PHOENIX: The Phoenix's dislike of financial matters is well compensated by the Sphinx. The Sphinx is both conservative and thrifty in their approach to most endeavours, and the Phoenix respects such attributes in others.

HATHOR: Hathors generally admire the clever Sphinx, whereas Sphinxes often find the romantic Hathor a stimulating companion.

THE SPHINX: Two Sphinxes tend to compete with one another, each out to get the upper hand. They are not argumentative by nature, and so this is unlikely to prevent successful, although unusual, relationships.

SHU: The openness of the Shu is appreciated by the Sphinx and the Shu is captivated by Sphinx inscrutability. However, the Sphinx can be a little too overbearing for the Shu.

FATE AND FORTUNE

Over the course of the year the Sphinx can expect the following influences to affect their lives during the separate Egyptian months:

THOTH 29 AUGUST – 27 SEPTEMBER:

The month of Thoth brings renewal to the Sphinx. Anything that seems to have reached a stalemate can be rejuvenated by the fresh possibilities of this month. If the Sphinx has become bogged down with a problem, the solution could present itself toward the end of this cycle. This is an especially favourable month for love, romance and affairs of the heart.

HORUS 28 SEPTEMBER – 27 OCTOBER:

If a Sphinx is looking for new employment this is a particularly positive time. Similarly, if the Sphinx is thinking of moving home an opportunity to relocate is very possible.

WADJET 28 OCTOBER – 26 NOVEMBER:

Wadjet acts as the message bearer for the Sphinx and news from a completely unexpected quarter may be received. The Serpent is a symbol of wisdom, and so the clever Sphinx is particularly astute during this month. Any arguments or disputes are likely to be resolved in the Sphinx's favour.

SEKHMET 27 NOVEMBER – 26 DECEMBER:

The Sekhmet month is a period favourable to any Sphinx involved in sport or other leisure activities, particularly regarding team events. Any team in which the Sphinx plays a major role is likely to triumph.

THE SPHINX 27 DECEMBER – 25 JANUARY:

The Sphinx is a thinker and often needs time to be alone. This is a month for the Sphinx to plan or merely to contemplate. If the Sphinx keeps a balanced perspective, and accepts the help of others, solutions to unresolved problems may be discovered.

SHU 26 JANUARY – 24 FEBRUARY:

The Shu month is a time when Sphinxes find answers where they least expect to find them. The Shu month is also a time of romance and adventure for the Sphinx.

ISIS 25 FEBRUARY – 26 MARCH:

The influence of the Isis month may be detrimental to the Sphinx. A headstrong and inflexible approach can cause problems, particularly in domestic affairs. This may be the best month for the Sphinx to take a vacation.

OSIRIS 27 MARCH – 25 APRIL:

This is another month when Sphinx opportunities are somewhat limited. Relationships may suffer if the Sphinx insists on having the upper hand. Business matters may also suffer if Sphinxes remain inflexible in their approach. However, if the Sphinx is prepared to see things from others' points of view, then profitable and rewarding changes of direction may result.

AMUN 26 APRIL – 25 MAY:

During the month of Amun all the Sphinx cunning will come into play. It is an especially productive time for business endeavours or matters connected with the professional environment. Promotion at work or recognition for achievements is very likely during this month. This is also a month of luck concerning chance endeavours.

HATHOR 26 MAY – 24 JUNE:

During the Hathor month the Sphinx will find acquaintances particularly helpful. If Sphinxes abandon their natural suspicion of strangers they will find many new avenues opened up to them.

THE PHOENIX 25 JUNE – 24 JULY:

In legend the Sphinx could easily outwit an opponent. Similarly most born in the Sphinx sign are capable of handling themselves in an argument. The resilient Phoenix, however, can rise majestically from defeat. During this month the Sphinx's usual eloquence may lead them nowhere. It is a time of considerable stagnation for the Sphinx.

ANUBIS 25 JULY – 28 AUGUST:

The Anubis month is well suited for romance in the Sphinx's life. Existing relationships may take on a new and interesting dimension, while new love affairs are possible for the Sphinx who is presently single.

SPHINX CORRESPONDENCES

STONE   QUARTZ
TREE   ALMOND
FOOD   WHITE GRAPES
HERB   CORIANDER
FLOWER   LILY

COLOUR   WHITE
LUCKY NUMBER   1
INCENSE   EUCALYPTUS
ANIMAL   LION
SYMBOL

FAMOUS SPHINXS
Kirstie Alley, Nicholas Cage, Jude Law, David Lynch, Marilyn Manson, Kate Moss.

SPHINX WORKING

O Hu,
Watcher of the Dawn
I call upon thee
Protect me from all ills that approach from the east.
Lord of Heliopolis
Protect me from all ills that approach from the south.
O Hu, Gatekeeper of the Silences
Protect me from all ills that approach from the west.

Great Lion, Guardian of the Rising Sun
Protect me from all ills that approach from the north.
O Hu, Lord of the Resting Places
Remain at all times about me
Tep-Neb-Rostau, Tep-Neb-Rostau, Tep-Neb-Rostau.
O Hu, Light on the Mighty River
When I cannot hear, lead me.
O Hu, Sentinel of the Gateway of the Duat
When I cannot see, show me the way
O Hu, Guardian of the Road to Rostau
Let me recognize and seize the opportunities that
    I am granted.

O Hu, Mighty One
Let thy hand work through me.
Guide me to my path of destiny.
Grant me now thy power.
Tep-Neb-Rostau, Tep-Neb-Rostau, Tep-Neb-Rostau.

CHAPTER 6

· SHU ·

26 JANUARY–24 FEBRUARY

May the breath of Shu bring life to the earth.
May his passing cleanse the sky.

From the Pyramid Texts.

Shu was the god of sunlight and air and as such was represented as a human being with his hieroglyphic sign, a feather, on his head. He was the brother and consort of the lioness-headed, Tefnut, and is therefore often referred to as one of the 'divine twins'. The Shu person has tremendous creative potential and once their true vocation is realized success is virtually guaranteed. Often, however, they are too self-conscious of their failures and ignore their achievements. When in difficulty there is also a strong tendency for Shus to withdraw, occupying themselves with a chosen pursuit which keeps them apart from others.

Shus are true romantics and love to fantasize and reminisce. Many share a marvellous talent to captivate an audience, enlivening conversation by their sheer enthusiasm for romance and adventure. The phrase 'still waters run deep' is often an apt description of the Shu. Indeed, many give the impression that somewhere within their souls there lies a myriad of divine secrets. Shus are natural performers and a flamboyant, dramatic personality never fails to win friends and gain influence. They enjoy a variety of interests and few will remain in the same job or social circumstances for their entire lives. Shus seldom do anything in a conventional style, but lend a showy, theatrical quality to their manifold ventures.

The helpful Shu is a valuable member of any group or team, always eager to offer assistance to associates. They bring fresh ideas and an individual approach with style and panache. Considerate and accommodating, Shus are prepared to lead by example. Shus hate discord and will avoid pointless quarrels at all costs. They much prefer to see those around them happy and content, and will go to great lengths to maintain harmony. They will, however, make a firm stand on behalf of friends, arguing their case with eloquence. Shus share a close affinity with nature coupled with a highly developed spirituality. They are compassionate and considerate and will try to alleviate suffering wherever it is found.

POSITIVE CHARACTERISTICS
A cheerful temperament makes most relationships easy for Shus and many enjoy considerable popularity. Love of social occasions is usual with much concern for the pleasure and happiness of others. Business capacity is well above average, although partners or colleagues are required to help with sound administration and investments. Most born in this sign have a deep sense of responsibility, generally sharing a conscientious and principled attitude to life.

NEGATIVE CHARACTERISTICS
Many Shus miss vital opportunities due to a hesitant and indecisive attitude. Until proved right or successful, Shus evidence a lack of confidence with too great a dependence on the opinions of others. Extravagance and a love of luxury can create financial problems. Sometimes Shus have unrealistic ideals or aspirations and

disappointments are bound to result. There is also a tendency for Shus to be possessive in relationships.

APPEARANCE

Those born in the sign of the Shu usually have long and graceful limbs. Endowed with a fine bone structure, the face of the Shu is warm and sensual. Their eyes are bright, alert and expressive, often with prominent lashes. They are agile, alert and elegant. Shu is a sign of elegance. The woman of this cycle seems almost to float or glide as she walks. The Shu man will have a purposeful and determined gait. Most Shu activity is conducted with deliberate and mindful composure: Shus refuse to sprawl or slouch even when relaxed.

HEALTH

The Shu is one of the healthiest of signs. Few born in this cycle will suffer from repeated bouts of colds or flu. Indeed, after childhood, viral infections of any kind are rare for Shus. Allergies are the most common complaints of this group. The Shu's highly active immune system can often result in such problems as asthma or hay fever. Many Shus suffer skin rashes, so often the consequence of nervous tension. Worry may result in headaches or nausea, particularly if the Shu is in distress.

WORDS OF ADVICE

The practicalities of life do not always fit well with the Shu's imaginative aspirations. Many have an unrealistic attitude to material pursuits and frequently suffer disappointment due to high expectations of relationships. Shus have wonderful humility and are seldom, if ever, arrogant or vain. Admirable though these qualities are, they may result in too much self-sacrifice and a lack of consideration for their own essential needs. Shus should make a determined effort not to let acquaintances walk all over them. Those born in this sign are sometimes too kind and generous for their own good.

SUITABLE OCCUPATIONS

The caring and understanding Shu works well with the underprivileged, the sick and the elderly. Their sympathetic nature, coupled with a willingness to listen to the problems of others, make counselling, psychology and social work ideal occupations. Shus are born communicators and anything entailing persuasion or requiring direct customer contact are also apt professions for Shus. Shus share a close affinity with nature and many are suited for work involving agriculture, conservation and animal welfare. With a natural flair for the dramatic, many Shus excel in careers concerning music, drama and dance.

THE SHU AT WORK

An amiable disposition brings the Shu popularity in the workplace. Colleagues can safely place their trust in the Shu. Anything told them in confidence is certain to remain a secret. They also provide a sympathetic ear for problems, and offer a firm shoulder on which to cry. Kind as they are, the accommodating Shu will not be afraid to speak up on behalf of workmates. They will, however, broach any complaint with considerable diplomacy, refusing to be sidetracked by anger or frustration. Shus are diligent and trustworthy workers, capable of intense devotion to duty. They prefer to work in their own way, excelling, so long as they are given ample scope for initiative. They are professionally ambitious, leaving no stone unturned to achieve their objectives. Shus do not work well under pressure, however, with a tendency to become forgetful when stressed.

THE SHU WOMAN

It is important for the Shu woman to feel good about herself. She will devote much time to her appearance and take great care of her health and fitness. It fills her with horror to think she may not look her best, and will never answer the door to anyone unless she is fully prepared. She even hates her closest friends to visit without warning. The woman of this sign is an elegant dresser. She is not a blind follower of fashion, however, but dresses in a style that suits her. In her opinion, if it does not happen to be the latest trend – so what! She is not the most domesticated of signs: her home will be clean and hygienic but often cluttered and untidy. The Shu woman is one of the most forgetful of any sign, forever mislaying her personal possessions.

The woman of this sign will frequently display an unorthodox attitude towards life and she lives according to their own set of rules and values. However, the Shu woman is always prepared to help those in distress. She is gracious and generous, an excellent listener and an amiable friend. She cannot abide gossip, however, refusing to continue with a conversation that turns to criticism of anyone not present. She loves company and is the perfect hostess. Indeed, she feels uneasy when alone, except, that is, when she is getting ready to go out – then she must be allowed to prepare in peace.

THE SHU MAN
Like his female counterpart, the Shu man will not seek to be the centre of attention. If pressed, however, he will rise to any occasion. Shu men hate inertia; they refuse to be bored under any

circumstances and are always searching for new ideas. Once anything becomes routine they look for something else to add to their list of interests. Sometimes they fail to acknowledge their own abilities, lacking faith in their talents and potential. At home the Shu man will often start with a job, such as painting and decorating or fixing the car, only to leave it unfinished. You can always tell the Shu man's house by a half-mown lawn or an abandoned piece of DIY.

The Shu is a born family man, surrounding his life with love and fellowship. He is one of the most devoted husbands and fathers of any sign, and so long as he has a secure environment to return to each evening he will excel in his chosen profession. He will work confidently with business colleagues and workmates alike, knowing precisely what he wants and how to achieve it. His strength of purpose comes from the knowledge that he is working for the benefit of his family. Indeed, if he were not giving his employers his very best he would feel he was letting them down. The Shu alone is a different matter. The Shu bachelor, for example, is often the most disorganised of any sign.

THE SHU PARENT

Shus are patient and tolerant parents. They do not believe in punishment or severe reprimand of any kind. Instead, they will let their children make their own mistakes, confident that it is the most valuable way for their offspring to learn. Shu parents are affectionate and loving and will encourage their young to the full, always giving the very best of advice. They like their children to be clean and tidy, however, but are rarely angry if they return home dirty or muddy from play. 'Kids will be kids', is usually the motto of the Shu parent.

THE SHU CHILD

The Shu is a sprightly and inquisitive child. They are also dreamers and often have invisible childhood friends. Indeed, Shu children will usually talk to themselves more frequently than other signs. That does not mean they do not have real companions: they forge friendships readily and enjoy considerable popularity with other children. They have such vivid imaginations that it is easy for them to create a colourful world of harmless make-believe.

From an early age Shu children are bright, alert and quick to learn, although they may require encouragement to perform well in school. Provided a subject is presented in a stimulating fashion, however, the Shu child will take to learning with great enthusiasm. It is up to teachers to make lessons interesting enough for the Shu to pay attention.

THE SHU FRIEND

Shus are special friends, good listeners and entertaining conversationalists, but they must share a common bond or affinity in order to enjoy close friendships. They are easygoing and hate to burden anyone with their own troubles. Shus refuse to judge their acquaintances, maintaining an open mind in most situations. They only have one failing as friends: they always mean to keep in touch with those who have moved away, but never seem to get around to it. Eventually, having failed to phone or write, they may even feel guilty and contact may sadly be lost for good.

Shus sometimes seem to exist in an insular, timeless world: they are always late for appointments, hate to be hurried, and insist on doing everything in their own good time. When working, thinking or preparing, Shus tend to talk to themselves. They are also garrulous in conversation, forever going off at tangents from the topic being discussed. Strangely enough, this can create a sense of shared reverie, having a remarkably calming influence on those who are anxious, worried or under stress. One always has the feeling that somehow everything will work out for the best after a chat with a Shu friend.

THE SHU PARTNER

Many born in the Shu sign are mellow and serene, capable of taking erratic or excitable partners in their stride. They exert a pacifying and calming influence on those in their vicinity. However, Shus are unlikely to be happy in close proximity to those who expect others to join them in a world of frenzied activity. They prefer to look, listen and learn, offering pertinent advice or comment at their own time of choosing, rather than be swept away with boundless enthusiasm.

The Shu lover is romantic and affectionate although sometimes a little too sentimental. They are open and giving and willingly offer their trust. They allow themselves to be captivated by those who bring adventure to their lives, providing it is not too disruptive. For the Shu to be at their best, they need a stable partner who has a responsible attitude to life. However, for the relationship to be truly successful, their partner must share an imaginative disposition. Moreover, anyone who lacks sensitivity is seldom attractive to those born in the Shu sign.

SHU AND OTHER SIGNS

AFFINITY SIGNS

OSIRIS: Many born in the Shu sign are calm and serene, well able to take the highly-charged Osiris in their stride.

THE PHOENIX: The Phoenix gets on best with those who are less active than they. Many born in the Shu sign are calm and serene – at least outwardly. Accordingly, they can exert a positive influence on the Phoenix's impulsive nature.

SHU: The unassuming Shu is usually happy in the company of other Shus. They have many common interests, experience few serious disagreements, and share a deep sense of intuition.

ANUBIS: The Anubis's strong family ties and protective instincts can make them ideal partners for Shus. Shus often look at life from a very different perspective to the Anubis, and their romantic imagination usually aids Anubis's creativity.

PROBLEM SIGNS

AMUN: The Shu is far too sensitive and emotional for the Amun, while the Amun is too overbearing for the Shu. The two signs have little in common, and their outlooks on life differ considerably.

HORUS: The serenity of lifestyle the Shu needs is unlikely to be found in close proximity to the Horus.

SEKHMET: The Sekhmet's energetic mentality is fascinating, though exhausting, to the peace-loving Shu.

OTHER SIGNS

THOTH: The Thoth is often attracted to the openness of the Shu, although the Thoth can mentally exhaust the Shu who prefers a more serene lifestyle.

HATHOR: Shus and Hathors both share an interest in the exotic and unusual aspects of life. Close friendships and relationships are possible, although marriage between these two signs can sometimes suffer due to a lack of practical considerations.

WADJET: Shus and Wadjets share little in common. However, this can sometimes lead to successful marriages. There is little for them to argue or disagree about.

ISIS: Shus are romantics by nature and may find themselves swept away by Isis panache. The Isis's lifestyle is often too dramatic for the Shu.

THE SPHINX: The openness of the Shu is appreciated by the Sphinx and the Shu is captivated by Sphinx inscrutability. However, the Sphinx can be a little too overbearing for the Shu.

FATE AND FORTUNE

Over the course of the year the Shu can expect the following influences to affect their lives during the separate Egyptian months:

THOTH 29 AUGUST – 27 SEPTEMBER:

Thoth brings favourable influences to bear on sporting and leisure activities. At social engagements Shus will be in their element. Positive developments in the course of the Shu's life could result from new acquaintances made during this month. This is an especially favourable period for love, romance and affairs of the heart.

HORUS 28 SEPTEMBER – 27 OCTOBER:

The Shu should be careful not to rush headlong into anything during the cycle of Horus. This month, however, can be an excellent time for the Shu to take a vacation.

WADJET 28 OCTOBER – 26 NOVEMBER:

Any Shu involved in academic pursuits will find that many achievements are made at this time of year. Shus may find that they are required to learn a new skill in order to obtain the best results from an important enterprise.

SEKHMET 27 NOVEMBER – 26 DECEMBER:

During the month of Sekhmet, Shus could experience difficulty in relationships. They will need their own space which others may not be prepared to allow them. The Shu should stand firm and refuse to be manipulated.

THE SPHINX 27 DECEMBER – 25 JANUARY:

The Sphinx is the message bearer for the Shu. Surprise news is likely in the early days of this month.

SHU 26 JANUARY – 24 FEBRUARY:

The Shu's own month is a positive influence for change. A move of location or occupation is particularly favourable at this time.

ISIS 25 FEBRUARY – 26 MARCH:

The Isis month is a time when Shus appear to have little control over their own affairs. However hard they try, they seem to get nowhere. It is often best for Shus to wait until the Isis month is over before they make important decisions.

OSIRIS 27 MARCH – 25 APRIL:

The Osiris month can be a time of laborious activity for the Shu. If lingering problems remain unsolved, this may be the time to act. The Shu has an especially practical attitude to life during this month, and is well placed to handle any difficulties that may previously have been avoided.

AMUN 26 APRIL – 25 MAY:

New ideas and intuitive inspiration can open many doors for the Shu. It is a favourable month for love and romance. Strangely, many Shus meet new partners, get engaged or even married during an Amun month.

HATHOR 26 MAY – 24 JUNE:

The Shu may find this a somewhat difficult month to handle. Combined, the influences of Hathor and Shu result in unrealistic or impractical enterprises. This is often a period when financial and domestic problems arise, while business affairs may also suffer.

THE PHOENIX 25 JUNE – 24 JULY:

The firebird brings much excitement to the Shu's life. Shus have a deeply romantic temperament and this month brings many opportunities through which romanticism may be channelled.

ANUBIS 25 JULY – 28 AUGUST:

It is a month when the Shu is especially lucky, particularly concerning ventures of chance. Business endeavours initiated at this time are likely to succeed and great reward is possible.

SHU CORRESPONDENCES

STONE   MOONSTONE

TREE   SILVER BIRCH

FOOD   LYCHEE

HERB   LEMON BALM

FLOWER   IRIS

COLOUR   PURPLE

LUCKY NUMBER   9

INCENSE   WHITE SANDALWOOD

ANIMAL   SWALLOW

SYMBOL

FAMOUS SHUS

Christian Bale, Drew Barrymore, Kurt Cobain, Sheryl Crow, Matt
Dillon, Minnie Driver, Natalie Imbruglia, Brandon Lee, Jennifer Jason
Leigh, Christina Ricci, Jerry Springer, Robbie Williams.

SHU WORKING

O Shu,
Bearer of the Sky
I call upon thee
Protect me from all ills that approach from the east.
Divine Twin, Lord of the Firmament
Protect me from all ills that approach from the south.
O Shu, Wings of the Silver Clouds
Protect me from all ills that approach from the west.
O Shu, Brother and Consort of Tefnut
Protect me from all ills that approach from the north.
O Shu, God of Light by Day and Moon by Night
Remain at all times about me.
Hinu-en-Shu-Nefer, Hinu-en-Shu-Nefer.
O Shu, Master of the Cool Winds and Breezes
When I cannot hear, lead me
O Shu, Conjuror of a Thousand Years
When I cannot see, show me the way.
O Shu, Lord of the Sun in Summer,
Let me recognize and seize the opportunities that
   I am granted.
O Shu, Sweet Swallow of Salvation
Let thy hand work through me.
Guide me to my path of destiny.
Grant me now thy power.
Hinu-en-Shu-Nefer, Hinu-en-Shu-Nefer.

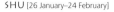

CHAPTER 7

· ISIS ·

25 FEBRUARY–26 MARCH

O blood of Isis, bring forth the great magic that will transform the world.

From the Egyptian Book of the Dead.

Usually represented in completely human form as a beautiful woman, the goddess Isis was worshiped as 'the great of magic'. Her name in Ancient Egyptian was Aset. As her name meant seat or throne, she was also the goddess of order. She was the symbolic mother of the pharaoh and the sister-wife of the god, Osiris and the mother of Horus.

Those born in this sign reflect the goddess's qualities in that they are both practical and intuitive in their approach to life. Isis can often see things from everyone's point of view. The Isis is endowed with an alert and appealing personality. Although outwardly calm and controlled, they harbour a wealth of inner emotion. Fully prepared to admit fault or error, the Isis has little reticence in changing their ideas or tactics should they be proved wrong. Able to accept criticism as an essential part of learning, most born in this sign will consider the opinions of friends and colleagues in all circumstances.

Those born in this sign review situations without personal prejudice, seldom choosing sides in disputes. Such admirable qualities permit them to formulate balanced plans and reach level-headed conclusions. The Isis will patiently look, listen and learn before deciding upon a course of action. Whether or not they agree with others, the Isis will try to appreciate the validity of all arguments. They are always ready to be persuaded – but reasoning must be sound.

The Isis is usually honest, forthright and idealistic. Both logic and intuition direct their actions – the perfect blend for success in any undertaking. They are hard-working and blessed with a keen, subtle intelligence, having little difficulty expressing themselves in a clear and eloquent manner. They mix well socially, are easygoing with their acquaintances and make undemanding friends and helpful colleagues. Isis people display imaginative foresight and have the remarkable aptitude to see things from varying perspectives. They will take all angles of a problem into consideration before arriving at conclusions, and are often inspired with revolutionary ideas.

POSITIVE CHARACTERISTICS

Isis people share an energetic, attractive and lively personality. A flamboyant character and a flair for the dramatic frequently make the Isis centre stage. Confident in most circumstances, the Isis has a unique talent to gain an overall perspective on any situation. A mystical inclination coupled with a highly developed sense of intuition turns many born in this sign toward philosophical or spiritual pursuits. Isis people are creative thinkers, having many unique and individual ideas. Imaginative and adaptable, a sense of humour affords them much social success.

NEGATIVE CHARACTERISTICS

Isis people have a vivid imagination and should problems become too serious they harbour a tendency to retreat into a world of make-believe. Lofty ideas may reduce the chances of success in practical ventures, while unrealistic expectations are a prime source of disappointment. Wishful thinking is also a danger in business affairs. Sometimes tactless, those born in this sign often speak their mind too readily.

APPEARANCE

Isis eyes are wide and expressive. Many born in this sign also have high foreheads and a well-defined widow's peak is not uncommon. They have quick reactions, although most move in a slow or deliberate manner. Everything the Isis does is undertaken with an appearance of calculated accuracy. Few born in this sign are likely to sprawl or slouch even when fully relaxed.

HEALTH

The Isis's intense commitment to projects and endeavours may result in anxiety and other stress-related problems. However, they regulate their lives in such a fashion that they are unlikely to suffer from gastronomic complaints or stomach trouble. One astonishing aspect of the Isis physiology is the capacity to heal or recover rapidly from injury. Broken bones mend quickly and cuts and bruises disappear in no time at all.

WORDS OF ADVICE

Idealists by nature, some born in this sign may prefer to live in a world of reverie, even fantasy, if problems become too serious. They may retreat from the dismal, uninviting world and become reserved, secretive and detached. In such circumstances the Isis must face reality and realise that everything is not always going to work out for the best. Another Isis drawback is a tendency toward compulsive devotion to work. For a heartfelt cause, they may devote themselves so entirely that relationships, family life and everyday matters are neglected. The Isis should remain aware of the potentially obsessive side to their character.

SUITABLE OCCUPATIONS

A thirst for knowledge draws many born in this sign into academic careers. An adventurous, enquiring mind equally suits the Isis to the world of scientific research. The Isis has an excellent eye for salient detail, so photography, painting, sculpture, architecture and commercial art are also appealing occupations for many born in this sign. The Isis enjoys the limelight. Whether actors, entertainers or professional persuaders, the Isis accurately gauges public reaction, capture attention and moulds opinion with considerable ease. Many successful advertising executives are born in the Isis sign.

THE ISIS AT WORK
The Isis has a flexible attitude to work. Their ability to see things from everyone's point of view ideally suits them for positions of responsibility. The Isis employer is a fair, conscientious and hard-working boss, while the Isis employee mixes well with colleagues. Few born in the Isis sign are found entangled in professional squabbles. They make excellent mediators, helping to solve any problems that arise in their place of work. The Isis's occupation must offer challenge and scope for initiative. If a job lacks stimulation or creative potential the Isis will soon grow bored and lose interest entirely. Until a fulfilling career is found, few born in this sign will remain content with a job for long.

THE ISIS WOMAN
The Isis woman is born in the most socially versatile of signs. She can converse eruditely at any level, be it at a formal banquet or in her local bar. She possesses a firm set of ideals and, no matter how

unconventional they may appear to others, she will defend them with zeal. The Isis woman insists on being treated on equal terms in male company. Brave is the man who dares to talk down to the Isis woman or treats her in a chauvinistic manner.

The Isis woman is a devoted friend, colleague and partner, though she may sometimes seem distant or preoccupied. She may also be changeable in temperament, one minute fully engrossed in conversation, the next detached in a world of thought. Acquaintances must learn to accept the Isis the way she is. There is no enmity in her behaviour: out of the blue, an idea completely removed from the current topic may simply have occurred to her.

Both male and females of this sign tend to adopt an unconventional style of dress. This is especially true of the Isis woman. Even if she is a dedicated follower of fashion, or needs to dress formally for work, she will always make an individual statement in her chosen attire. It may be no more than an unusual piece of jewellery, but look closely and somewhere about the Isis you will find her unique personal trademark.

THE ISIS MAN

Like the woman of this sign, mental privacy is of utmost importance to the Isis man and he will defend it with passion. He may also behave in an unorthodox manner, his motives inscrutable and complex. By contrast, those born in this sign are fascinated by the intentions and motivations of others. Be they friends, lovers or mere acquaintances, the Isis is determined to discover just what it is that makes them tick. The Isis man therefore has a paradoxical, enigmatic personality that many women find enchanting.

The Isis male is usually attracted to women who lead interesting or exotic lifestyles. At the very least they must share an unusual approach to life. To his partner he is kind and generous, but his lover must accept that, like his female counterpart, he will insist upon his own personal space – he just hates invasion of his private thoughts and contemplations. However, the Isis man seldom has anything to hide, he simply needs to retreat from time to time. Mental solitude enables him to solve not only his own problems but those of others.

THE ISIS PARENT

Isis parents will encourage their children to think for themselves and stand on their own two feet. They bring banal school subjects to life by injecting flair and imagination, making learning a more stimulating activity. Few born in this sign insist that their children adopt their own interests or values, neither will they reprimand their young without a fair hearing. Both Isis mothers and fathers alike will listen to their children eagerly and with an open mind before passing judgement on their motives or actions.

THE ISIS CHILD

Right from infancy, Isis children are dreamers, their ambitions high and their hearts overflowing with expectation. Isis children are constantly questioning the world about them, not satisfied until they have discovered the answer for everything that grabs their attention. Consequently, the young Isis may lack concentration in school, gazing through the classroom window at something more exciting outside. When they apply themselves, however, they are immensely creative achievers. Physical activity is not high on their list of priorities, even if they do have the physique to excel at sport. The Isis child much prefers to work alone rather than as part of an organized group or team.

THE ISIS FRIEND

The Isis is their own person, refusing to be drawn into any type of close-knit or elite community. They dislike conformity and prefer to remain an elusive but prominent figure in the crowd. The Isis enjoys socializing – they can be extremely witty, humorous and fun-loving – but they hate to confine themselves to one set of standards or principles. Everything has its place in Isis philosophy, and everyone has the right to their own opinions and lifestyle. Anyone who is dogmatic, inflexible or stuck in a rut is unlikely to be an Isis's friend. More than anything else, the Isis despises prejudice or injustice of any kind.

The Isis often experiences difficulty in making long-term friends, despite their engaging and magnetic personality. They are usually so different from others that they find it impossible to share continual enthusiasm for the same old routines. Once they do meet someone with whom they share a common outlook, the Isis can cast an irresistible spell on their new-found friend, leading them into a world of wonder and excitement. Furthermore, the Isis will do all in their power to protect those they love, sacrificing themselves should the need arise.

THE ISIS PARTNER

The young Isis often has unrealistic expectations of their chosen
partners and, more often than not, will encounter disappointment.
Eventually their attitude will adapt itself to reality and a compromise
attitude will be reached. Once committed, the Isis will be a devoted
and passionate lover, although public displays of affection are rare.
Successful marriages are possible so long as the Isis's partner allows
the Isis to retain their individualism and personal freedom. The Isis is
averse to interference in their affairs, no matter whom by or how
well intended.

Occasionally the Isis will seek temporary escape from the world. At
such times they will retreat and contemplate in solitude. Partners
may sometimes take this the wrong way, mistakenly believing that
they have done something to offend. Provided they are left to sort
out their problems alone, the Isis will soon return contented.

ISIS AND OTHER SIGNS

AFFINITY SIGNS

THE PHOENIX: In legend, once reborn, the Phoenix was impelled to fly to the temple of Heliopolis. Like the mythical bird, those born in the Phoenix sign will find themselves attracted to the exotic or unusual. The Isis is perhaps the most intriguing of signs, and their idiosyncratic style is irresistible to the Phoenix.

HATHOR: Hathors are often attracted to the unconventional Isis, while the Isis move towards those with imagination. These signs are most compatible, and many successful marriages and business partnerships result.

WADJET: The Wadjet love of learning is much respected by the Isis. The Wadjet finds the Isis's unique insight equally fascinating. The two signs work well together and marriages are often successful.

SEKHMET: Isis can take the energetic Sekhmet in their stride. The Sekhmet often needs a benevolent and controlling hand that the Isis is prepared to offer. Almost all the attributes lacking in both signs are compensated by the other, and some of the most successful marriages are formed between the Isis and the Sekhmet.

PROBLEM SIGNS

ISIS: Few born in this cycle are at ease in the company of others who share their sign. The Isis's life is often too unusual to be spent so close to another who has similarly unconventional attitudes.

THE SPHINX: The Isis is a sign that can solve the Sphinx's eternal riddle. Isis intuition gives them the ability to fathom the motives of those born in the cycle of the Sphinx. The Sphinx may find this acutely unnerving.

ANUBIS: The Isis can unnerve the Anubis. Few Anubis people like ideas as unconventional as those many born in the sign of Isis appear to share.

OTHER SIGNS

OSIRIS: The Isis needs their own space. The Osiris intends to be a part of everything too much for the Osiris's liking. Nevertheless, in Egyptian mythology Osiris and Isis were partners. As such, both can make considerable efforts to overcome their differences and long-lasting relationships are possible.

THOTH: Although the Isis and the Thoth mix well socially, relationships or business partnerships can suffer. When together, they tend to behave irresponsibly.

AMUN: The Amun admires the resourceful Isis, but the Isis often finds the Amun far too conventional in their approach to life.

HORUS: As both Horus and Isis commit themselves so completely to a chosen pursuit, these two signs work well together if they share a similar heartfelt interest. If their interests lie in different directions, however, they are unlikely to have the time to spare for one another.

SHU: Shus are romantics by nature and may find themselves swept away by Isis panache. The Isis's lifestyle is often too dramatic for the Shu.

FATE AND FORTUNE
Over the course of the year the Isis can expect the following influences to affect their lives during the separate Egyptian months:

THOTH 29 AUGUST – 27 SEPTEMBER:

This is a particularly favourable period for romantic affairs. Many Isis people first meet their future partners during the Thoth month. In business, the Thoth brings new opportunities for prosperity.

HORUS 28 SEPTEMBER – 27 OCTOBER:

Domestic matters are likely to play an important role in the life of the Isis during this cycle, and the home may need more attention than usual. This is a month of good luck concerning ventures of chance.

WADJET 28 OCTOBER – 26 NOVEMBER:

During the month of Wadjet the Isis could find themselves inadvertently drawn into problems over which they have no control.

SEKHMET 27 NOVEMBER – 26 DECEMBER:

The energetic Sekhmet positively influences the Isis. This is a particularly favourable time for sport and leisure activities. The Isis engaged in competition is especially likely to fare well.

THE SPHINX 27 DECEMBER – 25 JANUARY:

During the month of the Sphinx the Isis may acquire something they have long sought, only to discover it is not as they expected.

SHU 26 JANUARY – 24 FEBRUARY:

Shu brings social success for the Isis. If the Isis attends a special occasion during this month they could be in for a pleasant surprise.

ISIS 25 FEBRUARY – 26 MARCH:

During their own month the Isis is often inspired by unique and original ideas. Projects initiated during this cycle have far-reaching consequences. A change of lifestyle may be initiated.

OSIRIS 27 MARCH – 25 APRIL:

The month of the Osiris is a time of reflection and contemplation for the Isis. Outstanding problems may be resolved through Isis intuition. A new acquaintance may alter the course of the Isis's life.

AMUN 26 APRIL – 25 MAY:

This is the month when travel is favourable. Any Isis seeking change of home or occupation should discover new opportunities.

HATHOR 26 MAY – 24 JUNE:

The month of Hathor is a time for the Isis to plan. Any idea formulated during this cycle should lead to success. The influences of Hathor can easily be directed and channelled by the celestial Isis.

Any Isis seeking new relationships, especially in romance, could find this month particularly favourable.

THE PHOENIX 25 JUNE – 24 JULY:

During the Phoenix month the Isis often experiences greatest difficulty. Isis prefers one thing to end before another begins. Something the Isis had considered over and done with may return. An unwelcome connection with the past could open old wounds.

ANUBIS 25 JULY – 28 AUGUST:

Anubis and the Isis work hand in hand to ensure success. This is a month when hard work can finally pay off. Anubis is also the message bearer for the Isis, and surprise news is likely toward the end of this month.

ISIS CORRESPONDENCES

STONE   LAPIS LAZULI

TREE   SYCAMORE

FOOD   AVOCADO

HERB   TARRAGON

FLOWER   ROSE

COLOUR   GREEN

LUCKY NUMBER 7

INCENSE   LOTUS

ANIMAL   CAT

SYMBOL

FAMOUS ISISES

Chelsea Clinton, Patsy Kensit, Gary Oldman, Bruce Willis, Reese
Witherspoon.

ISIS WORKING

O Isis, Lady Aset
Mother of the Gods
I call upon thee
Protect me from all ills that approach from the east.
She of the Double Crowns
Protect me from all ills that approach from the south.
O Isis, Dweller in the House of the Evening
Protect me from all ills that approach from the west.
Great Goddess of the Golden Dawn
Protect me from all ills that approach from the north.
O Aset, Guardian of Dwellings
Remain at all times about me.
Aset Heru Ka Nekhet, Aset Heru Ka Nekhet.
Mother of the Horus of Gold
When I cannot hear, lead me.
O Isis, Lady of the Words of Power
When I cannot see, show me the way.
O Isis, Queen of Mesen, Giver of Life
Let me recognize and seize the opportunities that
*   I am granted.*
O Aset, Foremost among the Neteru
Let thy hand work through me.
Guide me to my path of destiny.
Grant me now thy power.
Aset Heru Ka Nekhet, Aset Heru Ka Nekhet.

CHAPTER 8

· OSIRIS ·

27 MARCH–25 APRIL

O Osiris, the eternally good, the perfect one,
he who sits in the place of the all-seeing eye.

From the Pyramid Texts.

Depicted in human form, with the insignia of rule, the crook and
flail, across his chest, Osiris was the god of the underworld and the
lord of the Nile. His name in Ancient Egyptian was Asar. Like the
evaporating waters of the Nile, those born in this sign tend to be
elusive. The Osiris is sometimes misunderstood and their emotions
are a mystery. They are highly active and, like the ever-flowing

waters of the river, those born in the Osiris sign rarely allow themselves to be restricted.

Most Osiris people are sprightly and quick-witted, and many born in this sign share a strong compulsion to keep on the move. Curious by nature, they show considerable interest in their friends' affairs and are ever ready to help or intercede on behalf of others. They are perhaps the most inquisitive of any sign – Osiris just hates to feel excluded. They are not natural followers, having an idiosyncratic style all their own. The Osiris is a mine of information. Even when they are discussing something of which they have little knowledge, they have the remarkable ability to make it seem as though they are experts. The Osiris is eager to impress and refuses to admit ignorance on any matter. They have a lively imagination and a remarkable talent to make life interesting for everyone.

Osiris is a sign of communication, and many born in this cycle share a love of language. They are voracious readers, erudite and eloquent, with the ability to express themselves in both a vivid and witty manner. They have a marvellous sense of humour although, unlike some signs, it is seldom zany or surreal. Neither is their humour unkind. They are unlikely to appreciate a joke at someone else's expense. Osiris people are natural communicators and others may find themselves captivated by their tales and anecdotes. Many Osiris people are excellent speakers with a natural ability to entertain and encourage others.

POSITIVE CHARACTERISTICS

Osiris people share an active intellect, together with a strong sense of intuition. Self-reliance and determination play an important part in ensuring Osiris success. Charm and personality arouse the interest of the opposite sex, while music and drama have much appeal. The Osiris has a highly energetic personality, coupled with keen powers of observation. Most are charitable and altruistic, although sometimes eccentric in their ways. They are fast on the uptake, quick to seize the initiative and are always eager for new experiences.

NEGATIVE CHARACTERISTICS

Often misunderstood, there is sometimes a need for the Osiris to avoid commitments and responsibilities. An intense dislike of bureaucracy and a refusal to conform to tradition sometimes results in avoidable complications in the Osiris's life. Although often gifted with a quick sense of humour, they are inclined to be cynical. The

Osiris also lacks tact when dealing with those they feel to be in the wrong.

APPEARANCE

Energetic by temperament, the Osiris seldom keeps still. Those born in this sign are particularly prone to gesticulating with their hands. Even on the phone, they make exaggerated gestures to emphasize a point or demonstrate what they are saying. Osiris is restless and fidgety, seldom seeming relaxed. When thinking, they are apt to doodle with a pen or pencil, or else fiddle with matches, pieces of paper or other small objects.

HEALTH

Osiris people are worriers, which may sometimes be detrimental to health. Allergies and ailments related to the nervous system are common complaints for those born in this sign. Not ones for routine, Osiris people have irregular eating habits and often skip meals. The positive effect is that they seldom have a weight problem. Alternatively, such a lifestyle can play havoc with the digestive systems. Osiris people dislike small or confined spaces and may suffer from claustrophobia: they particularly hate elevators or dark and tiny rooms.

WORDS OF ADVICE

Osiris people are noted for their adaptability and versatility. However, they tend to lack a singleness of purpose, and powers of concentration need deliberate cultivation. Otherwise, even though they have more creative potential than many other signs, they may not make the most of their talents. Osiris people generally spread themselves in too many different directions at one time and often fail to follow through what they started. No sooner something is under way than another, more interesting challenge is eagerly accepted. Osiris people should make longer-term plans – and stick to them.

SUITABLE OCCUPATIONS

Osiris people have keen powers of observation and are quick to learn. They are well suited for occupations that require fast reactions. They are not ideal candidates, however, for work necessitating long periods of intense concentration. They grow restless far too quickly. Teaching appeals to Osiris people, as does anything connected with the media. They are excellent talkers and Osiris people of both sexes are in their element as salespeople. They are not the best of listeners, however, and may fail to realize when they are falling short of persuading a potential buyer. They usually compensate by the sheer volume of work they can accomplish. Osiris people are happier in the open or away from headquarters. As white-collar workers they make better travellers, disliking the restrictions of the office environment. Similarly, in manual trades they work best on site. Osiris people can turn their hands to most endeavours, and intricate or inventive work has strong appeal.

THE OSIRIS AT WORK

Osiris people can accomplish many tasks simultaneously and are particularly industrious employees. As employers or in a managerial role they make a firm stand on major decisions. On lesser issues they are somewhat changeable, continually updating their strategy. Employees or fellow workers can be left confused by such Osiris tactics. All the same, their approach is one of adaptability that usually reaps reward. As fellow workers they are not always the easiest people with whom to get along. Some may find Osiris inquisitiveness annoying. Osiris people are always eager to keep up with gossip and sometimes say more than they should. Alternatively, they can be tremendous fun to be around, making the most laborious activities seem interesting.

THE OSIRIS WOMAN

For some, the Osiris woman makes a better sweetheart than a traditional kind of wife. She may be a devoted lover, but household chores she finds bothersome. She has no intention of spending hours washing, cleaning or preparing meals, although she will warmly welcome visitors to her home. Her usual response is 'take me as you find me'. The Osiris woman refuses to play the submissive wife. She will often insist on helping with the income, and is happiest when she too is a wage earner. Although somewhat untidy, she will treat her home as an efficient business, ensuring that the accounts are kept in order.

As a career woman, the Osiris is a conscientious worker. She is a marvellous organizer of business affairs, although somewhat sloppy, leaving everything lying around. Her desk is usually piled high with notes and other pieces of paper – a constant reminder of her busy schedule. Because the Osiris can easily handle numerous tasks simultaneously, many women born in this sign will continue with their chosen occupation once their children have reached school age. Most Osiris women also expect their husbands to share an equal responsibility in a child-caring capacity.

THE OSIRIS MAN

The Osiris man has a boyish air that is particularly attractive to the opposite sex. He is considerate to the opposite sex and treats them as equals. Most Osiris men fall for women with strong personalities, sometimes much older than themselves. Osiris people are somewhat untidy – Osiris men in particular. However, they always know precisely where everything is. If you tidy up after an Osiris man it can throw his life into turmoil.

Osiris men have plenty of charm. They can turn it on at will and are generous with the compliments. They are gifted with a quick or dry sense of humour and are always ready with a witty or pertinent remark. They usually share a frivolous attitude to life. When annoyed, however, they can be extremely sarcastic. Indeed, this is their usual means of defence. As a rule, the Osiris is a peace lover and unlikely to resort to violence. Indeed, they are so expert with their tongues that few Osiris men have the need to succumb to brawls. They do have a temper, however, but are inclined to take it out on the furniture or other inanimate objects. It is usually the Osiris man who smashes a plate or snaps a pencil when he has reached the end of his tether. Osiris people find a noisy way to express their anger, which accordingly releases tension.

THE OSIRIS PARENT

Osiris people are perhaps the most exciting parents for any child. They just love to be involved with their children's games. They wholeheartedly join in the fun, and are forever thinking up adventurous pastimes for their young. Holidays, in particular, can be full of adventure. The Osiris mother is young at heart and goes out of her way to follow her daughter's fashion – at least, as far as is feasible. The Osiris father similarly takes a keen interest in his son's activities – sharing a fishing trip or a visit to a ball game is a common joy for many men born in this sign. Sometimes children of an Osiris may find themselves embarrassed by their parent's enthusiasm, especially in front of their friends.

THE OSIRIS CHILD

Children born in this cycle are quick to learn, particularly to read. At school, Osiris children are often remarkable achievers, although they can be a bane for teachers. There will be few complaints concerning academic ability, but school reports may repeatedly criticize the Osiris's lack of concentration. The problem for many Osiris children is that they have usually understood the lesson early on and have grown restless and irritable while other children take time to catch up. The Osiris is also a worrier and sometimes examination results may suffer. As they are exceptionally keen to do well, children of this sign often overtax themselves on homework.

Osiris people are likely to succeed in life much earlier than many other signs. Indeed, many a child prodigy is born in this cycle. Their success in later life, however, depends very much upon controlling their inclination to chop and change the nature of their work. Osiris people find it hard to stick to anything for long, especially once it has become a matter of familiar routine.

THE OSIRIS FRIEND

The Osiris just hates to pass up a challenge and will often drop other commitments to pursue a new opportunity. On the other hand, those born in this cycle are the first to draw attention to the inconsistency of others. Another handicap for the Osiris is a tendency to become embroiled in petty details. Do not try arguing with an Osiris, however, it will get you nowhere – except into a state of confusion. The Osiris will have you skilfully sidetracked, just when you think you have proved a point.

Occasionally Osiris people show signs of jealousy, but this is usually only a temporary reaction. With frequently changing interests, they are quick to forget. If you seem to have offended the Osiris, you may be inclined to formulate a strategy to apologize. It usually isn't worth the bother. The Osiris has probably forgotten all about it. The best attitude to adopt with most born in the Osiris sign is live and let live.

THE OSIRIS PARTNER

Others will always know when the Osiris is annoyed. Partners will notice how they move noisily around the house, banging furniture or slamming doors. Sometimes Osiris people form deep attachments, at other times they move from one relationship to another with considerable ease. It may seem that they will never settle down, then suddenly, out of the blue, they announce they are about to marry. Generally, once the choice is made, they will work hard to ensure a lasting partnership – that is, provided their partner is prepared to accommodate the Osiris's manifold interests.

If a partner strongly disagrees with an Osiris's activities, the ideal strategy is to give it time. Before long, they usually find something else to do and quickly lose interest. Osiris people hate to be pressured. The best way to handle an Osiris is to air your objections and let the subject drop.

Osiris people love an evening with every romantic detail. Both Osiris men and women excel at dinner-table conversation, and both love to buy their partners gifts. The Osiris is one of the best signs with whom to share a date. In domestic life they can be somewhat irritating, however. They can never make up their minds about the colour of wallpaper or a new model of car. Even when they finally decide, they are forever complaining that they should have made a different decision.

OSIRIS AND OTHER SIGNS

AFFINITY SIGNS

SHU: Many born in the Shu sign are calm and serene, well able to take the highly-charged Osiris in their stride.

ANUBIS: Anubis people are prepared to give others their own space – something the Osiris desperately needs. Unlike some signs, the Anubis is usually an open book, having no problem with Osiris inquisitiveness.

HORUS: Both signs are particularly tolerant of one another. The Horus's shortcomings are similar to the Osiris's own, such as escaping wherever possible from tiresome responsibilities. Both hate to be tied down. With so many interests, the Horus is seldom in conflict with the Osiris.

OSIRIS: With so many interests, the Osiris is unlikely to find themselves in conflict with other of the same sign.

PROBLEM SIGNS

THOTH: The Thoth values privacy too much to be constantly around the Osiris. The Osiris often finds fault with Thoth changeability. Osiris people themselves are changeable, but in interests and activities: the Thoth is changeable in temperament.

HATHOR: The Hathor is too sentimental for the Osiris. The Hathor seeks close relationships and has a need for firm, emotional commitments. The Osiris feels too restricted by such demands.

THE SPHINX: The meticulous Sphinx can be most annoying to the Osiris. The two signs have markedly different temperaments and little in common.

OTHER SIGNS

ISIS: The Isis needs personal space. The Osiris intends to be a part of everything too much for the Isis's liking. Nevertheless, in Egyptian mythology Osiris and Isis were partners. As such, if both make an effort to overcome their differences strong relationships are possible.

WADJET: The Wadjet and the Osiris mix well enough, although close relationships are rare. Wadjets are too pragmatic and take life too seriously for the Osiris. Many Wadjets consider Osiris to be irresponsible.

SEKHMET: Sekhmets like to commit themselves to long-term endeavours. The Osiris is quickly irritated with anything that becomes routine or lacks variety.

THE PHOENIX: The Phoenix and the Osiris often work well together, although in relationships the Phoenix usually seeks consistency generally lacking in the Osiris's life.

AMUN: These signs often have many interests in common. However, the Osiris hates to be told what to do. The Amun is sometimes too authoritative for the Osiris's liking.

FATE AND FORTUNE

Over the course of the year the Osiris can expect the following influences to affect their lives during the separate Egyptian months:

THOTH 29 AUGUST – 27 SEPTEMBER:

Thoth is a sign of swift activity, while Osiris is a sign of quick thinking. As both are highly changeable by nature, the Osiris should be careful of making snap decisions.

HORUS 28 SEPTEMBER – 27 OCTOBER:

Horus is a sign of risk and courage, favourable for Osiris speculation. This is a month of adventure for the Osiris, and affairs of the heart can move in a positive direction. This is also a time of advantageous meetings and important new acquaintances.

WADJET 28 OCTOBER – 26 NOVEMBER:

Plans for change are best implemented during this cycle. Any Osiris seeking a new job or change of location may discover exciting possibilities.

SEKHMET 27 NOVEMBER – 26 DECEMBER:

The influence of the fire-breathing Sekhmet has a tendency to evaporate positive influences of the watery Osiris. Plans can be dashed and hopes and aspirations may seem to fade. The Osiris should tread carefully in domestic affairs; an innocent remark could be taken the wrong way.

THE SPHINX 27 DECEMBER – 25 JANUARY:

An intriguing mystery may confront the Osiris during the month of the riddle-guarding Sphinx. The Sphinx may also bring financial reward. It is a particularly lucky month for Osiris people, especially concerning games or sporting activities.

SHU 26 JANUARY – 24 FEBRUARY:

The month of the high-flying Shu is often a time of travel for the Osiris. It is a good month for a vacation or weekend away. It is also a time for favourable news.

ISIS 25 FEBRUARY – 26 MARCH:

This is a time for the unusual or unexpected. A word of warning, however – the Osiris should avoid taking everything at face value.

OSIRIS 27 MARCH – 25 APRIL:

During their own month Osiris people should be careful not to overwork. It is a time when haste could jeopardize business affairs or result in errors of judgement concerning finances. In matters of love and romance, however, the Osiris may be pleasantly surprised.

AMUN 26 APRIL – 25 MAY:

Amun is a sign of achievement in material affairs. It is also a sign of steady progress – requiring patience – and patience is not a Osiris virtue. Osiris people should not give up if something seems hopeless or slow in development. There is probably far more headway being made than they realise.

HATHOR 26 MAY – 24 JUNE:

The Hathor month can be a time of intense activity for Osiris people. They are more single-minded than at any other time of the year. This is usually a month of reward for a Osiris. New scope is often recognized by Osiris people at this time. An opportunity grasped during this cycle can often lead to great success. It is also a positive month for any Osiris seeking a new romantic affiliation.

THE PHOENIX 25 JUNE – 24 JULY:

The Phoenix: Osiris is a sign of fast, mercurial energy. The Phoenix is also a sign of rapidity, bringing progress for many Osiris people.

ANUBIS 25 JULY – 28 AUGUST:

Osiris people may find themselves entangled in quarrels or experience difficulty in relationships during the Anubis month.

OSIRIS CORRESPONDENCES

STONE	MOSS AGATE
TREE	CEDAR
FOOD	POMEGRANATE
HERB	BASIL
FLOWER	VIOLET

COLOUR	SILVER/GREY
LUCKY NUMBER	2
INCENSE	MYRRH
ANIMAL	SCARAB
SYMBOL	

FAMOUS OSIRISES

Patricia Arquette, Alec Baldwin, Robert Carlyle, Russell Crowe, Robert Downey Jnr, Sarah Michelle Gellar, Melissa Joan Hart, Lucy Lawless, Ewan McGregor, Shirley MacLaine, Haley Joel Osment, Quentin Tarantino, Christopher Walken.

OSIRIS WORKING

O Osiris,
Lord of the Two Plumes
I call upon thee.
Protect me from all ills that approach from the east.
Asar, Guardian of Souls
Protect me from all ills that approach from the south.
Great God, Whose Domain is the Duat
Protect me from all ills that approach from the west.
Lord Osiris, Lord of the Hidden Chest
Protect me from all ills that approach from the north.
Lord of Amenti, King of the Living
Remain at all times about me.
Khnemu-ut-em-Ankh, Khnemu-ut-em-Ankh.
O Asar, Sower of the Seeds of Time
When I cannot hear, lead me
Ye who dwells in Orion, with a season in the sky and a
    season on the earth
When I cannot see, show me the way.
Osiris, He of Two Thousand Years
Let me recognize and seize the opportunities that
    I am granted.
Great God, Lord of Right and Truth
Let thy hand work through me.
Guide me to my path of destiny.
Grant me now thy power.
Khnemu-ut-em-Ankh, Khnemu-ut-em-Ankh.

CHAPTER 9

· AMUN ·
26 APRIL–25 MAY

O Amun, hidden one, he who abides in all things, he who rules over all.

From an inscription at the Temple of Karnak.

Sometimes represented with the head of a ram, sometimes in completely human form, Amun became the supreme state god during the Late Kingdom of ancient Egypt. He was the highest creator god, who brought the cosmos into existence, creating the earth and sky from the power of his thoughts. Those born in this sign are strong and resolute, others looking to them for guidance. The Amun person, however, can often fail to understand those less strong, finding it incomprehensible that the tasks they find easy others may find hard. They make excellent leaders, so long as they remember not to overtax their followers. If left without a challenge, the Amun may lapse into a state of lethargy, content to watch the world go by. They are not the best people in the world to initiate a project, although once underway Amun leadership traits afford an invaluable contribution towards success.

Particularly conscientious concerning most endeavours, the Amun often plays a leading role in political organisations or social groups. Few born in this sign are inclined to do anything on the spur of the moment and most are averse to change. The Amun forms firm opinions and convictions. Anything to which the Amun's mind is set is well within the realms of possibility. They have a practical attitude to life and are seldom ones for dreaming, reminiscing or fantasizing. The Amun is a realist and most born in this sign have an abundance of common sense.

Amun types have much patience, and most Amuns apply themselves with continual diligence to any enterprise. In business matters Amuns make excellent spokespeople, able to negotiate the best bargain. The Amun, however, is not the ideal sign for initiating a new project, being suspicious of the risks involved. Experimentation is not an Amun trait, and most born in this sign are reluctant gamblers.

POSITIVE CHARACTERISTICS
Amuns have exceptional powers of leadership and strong willpower is matched by excellent executive skills. With considerable ability for making money, the Amun is always willing to devote time and effort towards the success of an enterprise. Strongly principled, they often possess great courage and are reliable and trustworthy. With much physical vitality, they usually enjoy robust health, coupled with a love of sport, action and outdoor activities.

NEGATIVE CHARACTERISTICS
An overbearing attitude may reduce the chances of social success, while a headstrong temperament, matched by intolerance, can lead to conflict. Errors of judgement are sometimes made due to strongly biased opinions. Many Amuns share unrealistic expectations of others and stubborn adherence to ideas can make certain relationships difficult. Sometimes the Amun can be arrogant and overbearing.

PHYSICAL APPEARANCE

Those born in this sign are often sturdy in appearance, have firm features and share a confident and authoritative stature. The Amun usually looks you straight in the eyes while exuding a powerful countenance. However, although this is a sign of activity, it is not a sign of nervous energy. There may therefore be a tendency towards overweight, particularly in later life.

HEALTH

Throat infections are common for those born in this sign, especially in childhood when frequent bouts of tonsillitis are usual. As the Amun is a physically active sign, injuries and broken limbs are common amongst this group. Some signs may be slim, even skinny, no matter what their lifestyle. The Amun, however, needs to make a concerted effort regarding diet or exercise to remain trim.

WORDS OF ADVICE

Amuns are often over-cautious and share a stubborn reluctance to take chances. They may be highly competent organizers and administrators, but experimentation and risk taking is best left to others. Sometimes their hesitancy can be a handicap: frequently they fail to exploit their capabilities or realize their full potential.

They often become set in their ways, finding it difficult to adapt to new situations. For the best results, the Amun should learn to take the occasional risk and realize that failures are often an important part of learning.

SUITABLE OCCUPATIONS

Amuns prefer occupations offering steady advancement and long-term security. Their enviable patience sees them through times of difficulty, usually leading to supervisory or managerial roles in their chosen line of work. Those born in this cycle are good with money so financial careers have considerable appeal. Amuns make excellent bankers, although work involving financial speculation is not the forte of the cautious Amun. Amuns are usually successful in whatever occupation they chose. They make sensible and responsible decisions in management and are conscientious workers. The Amun is a versatile sign regarding employment and most born in this cycle are quite capable of learning almost any trade.

THE AMUN AT WORK

The Amun is a sign of fixed character: few born in this cycle have adaptable personalities. If a change in outlook or direction is required in their working environment, the Amun may find it hard to adapt. Amuns are consistent in outlook, habits and behaviour, and pursue a professional objective with continual application and dedication. They make the most steadfast of colleagues and fellow workers generally know exactly where they stand with the Amun. They are easy enough to get along with during working hours, but Amuns like to draw a strict dividing line between working and social life. Often their personal friends are from an entirely separate circle of acquaintances to their colleagues at work.

THE AMUN WOMAN

The Amun is both an industrious career woman and a committed home-maker. Unlike some signs, however, she may find difficulty mixing the two. The happiest Amun is often she who has devoted her life to one or the other. Most Amuns dislike having to constantly change hats during the course of their life.

At work and in home life alike, the Amun woman enjoys organization. She is keen to ensure that everything runs smoothly during social or business occasions and commits herself accordingly. Those born in this sign like to feel secure in their surroundings, so the Amun woman always looks the part. Uneasy standing out in a crowd, she will generally wear what is right for the occasion.

The Amun woman will take a central role in social activities. She is always ready to give advice and is often the best shoulder on which to cry. Her own problems, however, she keeps to herself, being the last to worry others with her own concerns. It is so difficult to tell what the Amun woman is thinking or, more importantly, how she is feeling. Like her male counterpart, unless angered, the Amun woman keeps her emotions very much to herself.

THE AMUN MAN

The Amun man is brave and courageous, usually in command of most situations. Circumstances where he might experience difficulty, he usually avoids from the outset. He is confident, consistent and his response to most problems is calm, controlled and effective. However, like the woman of this sign, Amun men have a nasty temper if pushed too far. Most activities the Amun undertakes in a precise and methodical way. A man of regular habits, the Amun is the last person to cause surprise with uncharacteristic behaviour. Although he may be somewhat predictable, he is good-humoured and an excellent

conversationalist. With the opposite sex he is always the perfect
gentleman and his manners are impeccable.

The Amun is not a man to make large numbers of casual
acquaintances, preferring instead a small circle of close friends. He
is disturbed by company not of his choosing, and often prefers to
socialize with his own acquaintances rather than those of his
partner. Accordingly, Amun wives sometimes find themselves
isolated in marriage. Another problem for Amun wives can be the
mother-in-law. Amun men often remain extremely attached to their
mothers, sometimes allowing them to influence their lives a little too
much.

Like his female counterpart, the Amun man keeps a strict account of
his money and economizes whenever possible. All the same, he will
always make certain that he drives the best car that he can afford –
status symbols are particularly important to the Amun man.

THE AMUN PARENT

Home life means a great deal to the Amun, and family roots run
deep. Amuns are one of the most caring signs when it comes to the
welfare of their children, although emotionally they may be

somewhat restrained. They will encourage their young in their schoolwork, but may be unresponsive to their personal problems. Typically Amuns feel that others will be as strong as they and so tend to lack sympathy with those in emotional crisis. 'Just forget about it,' might be an easy solution for the Amun, but others are not so strong. However, Amuns always make certain that their children are well dressed, fed and cared for, no matter what personal sacrifices are necessary to make.

THE AMUN CHILD

From a very early age the Amun child will be a responsive and eager learner. Amun children are inquisitive in the extreme, wanting to know the reason – the full reason – for everything. They are seldom put off with a half answer. They work diligently at school and usually do well in class. There are seldom bad reports for the Amun child. They are keen to succeed in sports and many school captains are Amuns.

Amuns prefer routine and dislike change. A new school or move of home can considerably upset the young Amun. Providing that their surroundings remain consistent, the Amun child is usually easy to please.

The Amun has a constructive attitude to life and few Amun children will deliberately cause trouble or break their toys. They are particularly polite to adults but there is a tendency for the Amun child to be overbearing with other children. They are seldom bullies, although they usually insist on taking the lead with their friends.

THE AMUN FRIEND

Amuns are peace loving and amiable, wishing to live in harmony with their associates and neighbours. Few Amuns are responsible for causing trouble of any kind. When annoyed, however, they have quite a temper. Beware of trying the patience of the Amun. Once hurt or angered, the Amun is slow to forgive and will never forget. They make loyal and supportive friends, but bad enemies.

Both male and female Amuns are somewhat possessive in relationships and friendships alike. They choose their acquaintances carefully, making sure they mix with others who share their beliefs and sentiments. Accordingly, there are seldom conflicts of interest. However, if one of their friends should change their attitudes or find others with whom to spend more time, the Amun may feel personally insulted. Amuns make devoted friends but are uneasy about casual acquaintances of any kind.

THE AMUN PARTNER

Both Amun men and women are passionate and uninhibited lovers, although romantic sentiment is not a natural Amun trait. Keen to establish order and routine in their lives, they tend to marry young. This can sometimes lead to hasty decisions. In fact, marriage is about the only time in the Amun's life when they do not think long and hard about a commitment. If the right partner is found, the Amun will do everything they can to ensure that the marriage succeeds.

The Amun enjoys flattery and admiration, particularly from the opposite sex. This sometimes results in wrong impressions. The fact that both Amun men and women are inclined to innocent flirtation can lead their partners to believe that they are being unfaithful. This is seldom true of the Amun: they are usually the most loyal partners of any sign.

Those born in this cycle are especially hurt when a relationship fails. Break-ups demoralize the Amun considerably and their entire life may suffer as a result. When a relationship ends the Amun sees it as a personal failure. Amuns have considerable difficultly coping with turmoil or coming to terms with change.

AMUN AND OTHER SIGNS

AFFINITY SIGNS

SEKHMET: The industrious and optimistic Sekhmet is admired by the Amun. Both signs share the ability to consistently devote themselves to a single objective or goal.

THE SPHINX: The Sphinx is the sign that the Amun often admires the most. Their ability to make something out of nothing, together with their keen financial instinct, are greatly respected by the Amun.

WADJET: Wadjet is a sign of wisdom and those born in this cycle are particularly creative concerning practical endeavours. The Amun is a materialist and so the two signs complement one another. Both signs lead similar social lives and close friendships and attachments are common.

PROBLEM SIGNS

SHU: The Shu is far too sensitive and emotional for the Amun, while the Amun is too overbearing for the Shu. The two signs have little in common, and their outlooks on life differ considerably.

THOTH and THE PHOENIX: The Amun likes consistency. Both these signs are too erratic by far.

HATHOR: The Hathor hates being controlled, while Amuns love being in control.

OTHER SIGNS

OSIRIS: These signs often have many interests in common. However, the Osiris hates to be told what to do. The Amun is sometimes too authoritative for the Osiris's liking.

HORUS: The Horus is a particularly affectionate sign, and the Amun tends to distrust open displays of affection. The Amun, however, can sometimes provide an emotional balance for the Horus.

ANUBIS: Anubis and Amuns mix well socially as both are polite and confident signs. When working together, however, there can be clashes of interest. In marriage there may be problems as both signs are exceptionally stubborn.

AMUN: Amuns get on great with Amuns of the opposite sex. They both love order and consistency in a relationship. Amuns of the same sex, however, tend to clash.

ISIS: The Amun admires the resourceful Isis, but the Isis often finds the Amun far too conventional in their approach to life.

FATE AND FORTUNE
Over the course of the year the Amun can expect the following influences to affect their lives during the separate Egyptian months:

THOTH 29 AUGUST – 27 SEPTEMBER:
Thoth is a sign of movement, change and versatility. The Amun is sometimes loath to change direction. During this month, however, they may be impelled to rethink a strategy. Whether a business or domestic affair, a decision requiring a new approach needs attention. The Amun should beware of expecting everything to remain the same. Any Amun considering a change of work or location may find it profitable to start their search at this time.

HORUS 28 SEPTEMBER – 27 OCTOBER:

During the month of Horus the Amun should make time for relaxation. Sport and other leisure-time activities are favourably placed, and vacations taken during the cycle of Horus can be especially fulfilling for the Amun.

WADJET 28 OCTOBER – 26 NOVEMBER:

The wise Serpent brings contemplation to the Amun. At this time of the year the Amun may become somewhat withdrawn in social circumstances. Relationships, particularly with colleagues or close friends, may suffer.

SEKHMET 27 NOVEMBER – 26 DECEMBER:

Domestic matters may require much of the Amun's attention. The Amun should try to divide their time equally between work, rest and play. Unusual occurrences around the end of this month may bring a radical change in everyday affairs. This is often a favourable month for love, romance and affairs of the heart.

THE SPHINX 27 DECEMBER – 25 JANUARY:

The Sphinx month is often a time of conundrum, and complex circumstances are likely to confront the Amun. Friends, relatives or work colleagues will be particularly helpful and may even provide solutions to longstanding problems the Amun has been unable to resolve. The Sphinx acts as the message bearer for the Amun. Surprising news can be expected around the end of this month.

SHU 26 JANUARY – 24 FEBRUARY:

The airy Shu and the earthy Amun are signs often worlds apart. This may be a time of little change in the Amun's life.

ISIS 25 FEBRUARY – 26 MARCH:

It is often during the Isis month that the Amun will act completely out of character. Based simply on intuition or instinct, the Amun may make an inspired decision. A new enterprise or relationship forged during this cycle is likely to bring considerable reward for the Amun.

OSIRIS 27 MARCH – 25 APRIL:

This may be a time of considerable frustration for the Amun. Osiris is a sign of intangibility and the Amun dislikes anything they cannot pin down. In the Osiris month Amuns may find it particularly difficult to get to grips with the circumstances surrounding them.

AMUN 26 APRIL – 25 MAY:

The Amun should be careful during their own month. They should give and take a little more and accept that not everything is going to go to plan. Others have their own ideas that the Amun should take into consideration. If the Amun lets circumstances be as they are, this can be an extremely favourable month for romance.

HATHOR 26 MAY – 24 JUNE:

This is a time of financial reward for many Amuns. Good news, especially concerning monetary matters, is to be expected. The Amun is not a gambler by nature, but a risk taken during this cycle is likely to be rewarded.

THE PHOENIX 25 JUNE – 24 JULY:

Many Amuns find the renewing Phoenix bring them fresh opportunities, particularly of a financial or business nature. Affairs of the heart may be problematic, however, due to a tendency by the Amun to apply themselves too much to material matters.

ANUBIS 25 JULY – 28 AUGUST:

Anubis is the Amun's most favourable period for romance and adventure. Amuns seldom let themselves be carried away by emotion. They may have little choice during this particular cycle. Any Amun looking for a new love in their life may also be pleasantly surprised during this month.

AMUN CORRESPONDENCES

STONE	TURQUOISE
TREE	OAK
FOOD	DAMSON
HERB	SAGE
FLOWER	BLUEBELL

COLOUR	BLUE
LUCKY NUMBER	4
INCENSE	CLOVES
ANIMAL	RAM
SYMBOL	

FAMOUS AMUNS

Fairuza Balk, Cate Blanchett, Bono, David Boreanaz, Pierce Brosnan, Naomi Campbell, George Clooney, Penelope Cruz, Kirsten Dunst, Tim Roth, Uma Thurman.

AMUN WORKING

O Amun,
Father of the Gods
I call upon thee
Protect me from all ills that approach from the east.
O Amun, Lord of the Hidden Abode
Protect me from all ills that approach from the south.
King of the Four Horizons
Protect me from all ills that approach from the west.

O Permanent One, King of the Setting Sun
Protect me from all ills that approach from the north.
O Amun, Eternal Flame of Life
Remain at all times about me.
Asha Renu, Asha Renu, Asha Renu,
He who is rich in names.

When I cannot hear, lead me.
O Amun, Dweller on the Throne and Keeper of the Sceptre
When I cannot see, show me the way.
O Amun, Hidden of Aspect, Mysterious of Form
Let me recognize and seize the opportunities that
    I am granted.

Great God, Maker of the Two Lands
Let thy hand work through me.
Guide me to my path of destiny.
Grant me now thy power.
Asha Renu, Asha Renu, Asha Renu.

CHAPTER 10

· HATHOR ·

26 MAY–24 JUNE

May I, in the following of Hathor, be inspired to create in her name.

From a tomb inscription at Thebes.

Usually the goddess Hathor was depicted in human form wearing on her head the sun-disc flanked by a cow's horns, but she was sometimes portrayed in the form of a white cow. He name in Ancient Egyptian was Het-Hert. She was both a goddess of the land and of the sky, and had strong associations with love, music and dancing. As such, this is a sign of grace and charm.

Usually possessing great artistic flair, the Hathor does not accept art for its own sake, seeking instead practical applications for their creations. Hathors may get carried away with enthusiasm, but they work best if they control and direct their creativity. Once they discover a balance between the down-to-earth and the imaginative, those born in this sign are free to accomplish outstanding achievements. Many Hathors have both spiritual and material aspirations. It is as though they have a foot in two worlds. Although they are highly imaginative, most Hathors are realists and few are content to live in a world of make-believe. Their intuitive decisions are often implemented with firm, rational logic.

If circumstances are working in their favour Hathors can be outgoing and extrovert. Conversely, if they do not have the right support or encouragement they are prone to become shy and retiring. Generally, they enjoy being the centre of attention. Even the shy Hathor will indirectly compensate: even if they spend much of their time in seclusion, their work ensures their fame.

The strongest motivation for the Hathor is to be able to enjoy life to the full. They have the enviable knack of living well, even if they have little money. Those born in this sign are experts at obtaining the best from most situations. Hathors have a generous nature and gain much contentment from helping others. If those around the Hathor are happy, so are they.

POSITIVE CHARACTERISTICS

Having natural charm, the Hathor is both expressive and theatrical. With easily stimulated emotions, they have tremendous enthusiasm for new ideas. They share an originality of thinking with a quick intellect and good memory. The Hathor has the capacity to learn easily. They have a romantic temperament coupled with great love of travel and adventure. Neat and tidy, the Hathor takes pride in their personal appearance.

NEGATIVE CHARACTERISTICS

Impatience and intolerance often result in considerable frustration and difficulties arise mainly through restlessness. For those born in this sign there is a tendency to fly to extremes and irritability can strain relationships. Hathors have strong likes and dislikes and their emotions are easily aroused. They are often impulsive by nature and extravagance is sometimes a problem. Envy is a Hathor trait, and jealousy needs to be controlled.

APPEARANCE

The typical Hathor has sensitive features with large, expressive though sometimes sorrowful eyes. Although alert and active, most Hathors are graceful in their movements. Hathor women have a sensual appeal, while Hathor men tend to be smooth and sophisticated. The facial features of both are particularly expressive.

HEALTH

Strangely, many Hathors have problems with their feet and breaking in new shoes can be agony. They are particularly vulnerable to colds and flu, after which many suffer from lingering coughs. Bronchitis and other chest complaints are common for Hathors, particularily if they are smokers. On the positive side, few Hathors suffer from digestive complaints; ulcers are rare for those born in this sign.

WORDS OF ADVICE

Hathors find it difficult to run their lives on simple, well-organized lines. They often find themselves in difficult predicaments, usually due to good intentions and a tendency to expect others to act as considerately as they. Although generous, the Hathor has a self-indulgent streak. If life is not full of variety and stimulation they soon grow bored. They may forget their obligations and move on to new endeavours. Hathors also lack willpower, needing the moral support of others to achieve success. They are especially sensitive to adverse opinion and may admit defeat simply because someone else has told them that something will fail. Although they are strongly individualistic, they are anything but loners. Hathors need encouragement of friends and associates – they are prone to stagnation and misery if left without support. Although it might be difficult, Hathors should try to have more faith in themselves.

SUITABLE OCCUPATIONS

Intuition, imagination and versatility are Hathor qualities, and many born in this sign achieve the best results once they have discovered an application for these traits. Ideal occupations for Hathors are those offering scope for their artistic talents. The Hathor is one of the most imaginative signs and many excel in all branches of the arts. Dancing, singing, acting and drama have strong appeal. The more retiring Hathor may concentrate on painting, writing or sculpture, which allows them to be apart from others for much of their time. Their much-needed appreciation comes via the appeal of their work. Most Hathors commit themselves to the good of others, so social work and health care have strong appeal. Many Hathor women make excellent child minders or careers for the sick or elderly. Hathor men are often found involved in youth schemes and other forms of community work.

THE HATHOR AT WORK

The Hathor can be most misleading. A shy Hathor will be strong and motivated in times of crisis, whereas the tougher Hathor will be a real softie inside. Work colleagues are often surprised by the Hathor who suddenly displays abilities or talents they least expected. It is a mistake for any prospective employer to readily categorize the Hathor, especially during an interview. What you see is not all you get with the self-conscious Hathor. Hathors may not handle their own affairs with the thrift of some signs, but when it comes to business matters they have a good head for profit.

THE HATHOR WOMAN

The Hathor woman is a great conversationalist and an eager listener and her company is much appreciated by men. Even the shy Hathor has an entertaining countenance when apart from the crowd – she too enjoys much attention. Many women envy her popularity and accordingly she may experience some difficulty in making close female friends. Many Hathor women who continue in work after starting a family will do so in a self-employed capacity. They are particularly astute regarding style and fashion, and many beauty consultants are Hathor mothers in part-time work.

The Hathor woman is neat and tidy, although she is far more concerned with her personal appearance than with the state of her home. She usually spends so much time concentrating on her hair, clothes and make-up, that housework is often left unattended. It can come as a complete shock for a first-time visitor to a Hathor woman's home – her personal living space is nowhere near as orderly as they expected. Hathor woman prefer particularly feminine fashions. Soft shades are often her choice of colours, while jewellery is small, delicate and tasteful.

THE HATHOR MAN

Hathor men are cool, calm and collected, and usually the centre of attention. Like his female counterpart, he is popular with the opposite sex, and others may be jealous of the attention he receives. He is not a fast-fire talker, however, and his sense of humour leaves something to be desired. Instead, he has a smooth-talking charm that usually appeals to women rather than men. Few Hathor men are boisterous or vulgar in mixed company, and their refinement may exclude them from many 'manly' activities.

The Hathor man may play an active role in sport and leisure pursuits, but he works best in a leadership or organizing capacity rather than as 'one of the boys'. Many Hathor men have an interest in politics, and the trade-union movement includes a considerable number of Hathors in active roles. With his partner, the Hathor man will be gallant and accommodating, if not a little old fashioned. He will treat his lover like a lady, and cannot resist buying her chocolates and flowers. In today's world many women regard such behaviour as condescending and may even consider the Hathor a chauvinist. Others who adore being so treated may discover that a date with the Hathor man can be most romantic.

THE HATHOR PARENT

Many Hathors enjoy strong family ties. The more people to love and be loved by, the happier they are. In many ways Hathor parents may be a little too lax with their children. They strongly disapprove of punishment of any kind, preferring instead to reward their children for success rather than scold them for failure. Hathors are one of the best signs for comforting a child who has failed an examination, is experiencing difficulty at school, or is in distress of any kind. Many Hathors spoil their children rotten.

THE HATHOR CHILD

So often a gentle, loving child, the sensitive Hathor needs much encouragement to face the harder realities of life. The romantic painting of the tearful, wide-eyed orphan, so popular in Victorian times, often epitomizes the Hathor child. They are dreamers and many have invisible childhood friends. Even those that do not will regularly talk to themselves and many will spend hours playing alone.

Hathor children mature later than those of other signs. Sometimes this means that they are bullied or badgered by older kids. In their teens, however, they quickly learn to stand up for themselves. Hathors are not aggressive by nature and many abhor physical violence. When absolutely necessary, however, they are quite prepared to meet like with like.

Hathor children are especially creative and many excel in the arts. The sciences, however, seldom appeal to the Hathor child. Teachers may complain about their performance in subjects like mathematics, chemistry or physics. Few children born in this sign pay much attention to lessons in which they have absolutely no interest.

THE HATHOR FRIEND

There is a mercurial quality about the Hathor that often confuses friends. Unconsciously, Hathors can adopt the attitudes, habits and mannerisms of those with whom they are closely associated. This is one reason that Hathors are so popular with the opposite sex – they can be all things to all people.

Although Hathors enjoy flattery and attention, most retain a genuine modesty regarding their work. Indeed, some find it hard to accept praise for their professional achievements. Again, this can be confusing to Hathor friends, who may wonder if they have somehow offended them with a heart-felt compliment. Hathor modesty is genuine, although some of their reactions are not. They are natural actors, not above feigning enthusiasm for something in which they have no real interest. The Hathor may seem riveted with your conversation, when all the time they are actually bored stiff. Hathors are especially polite and hate to offend. They have, however, no intention of going through the same experience twice.

THE HATHOR PARTNER

The personal life of the Hathor would provide rich material for the romantic novelist. Falling in and out of love is a regular habit for those born in this sign. Hathors share an idealistic, if not unrealistic, attitude to romance. Even if a relationship ends in disaster, the Hathor remains eternally optimistic about future affairs. They seem to believe that love is exactly as it is in the movies. If a relationship fails to blossom they are often deeply hurt, and usually blame themselves. Hathors, however, are not possessive lovers and few will continue to throw unwanted attentions in an ex-partner's direction.

Hathors enjoy romance to the extent that marital commitments seldom come early. When they eventually do settle down, it is generally the Hathor's partner who takes the lead. Hathor's husbands are expected to pull their weight with the housework, while Hathor's wives are usually left to handle all domestic affairs. Hathor women, in particular, seem to get their partner to do exactly what they want – at precisely the right moment they can turn on the tears or charm.

Though vulnerable to passing infatuation, the Hathor is capable of considerable loyalty. If love begins to fade, however, Hathor fidelity will soon follow suit. The Hathor hates to hurt another's feelings, and sometimes they find it difficult to terminate one affair before another begins.

HATHOR AND OTHER SIGNS

AFFINITY SIGNS

THOTH: The Hathor particularly enjoys the company of the Thoth. The Hathor's romanticism is often inspired by the Thoth's adventurous spirit.

THE PHOENIX: The Hathor likes the company of the Phoenix. Both have a romantic temperament that can inspire each another to achieve great success.

ANUBIS: Anubis and Hathor are particularly compatible signs, especially concerning romantic affiliations. Both share common interests, although their personalities are sufficiently different not to clash.

ISIS: Hathors are often attracted to the unconventional Isis, while Isis types move towards those with imagination. These signs are most compatible, and many successful marriages and business partnerships result.

PROBLEM SIGNS

AMUN: The Hathor hates being controlled, while Amuns love being in control.

HATHOR: The Hathor does not find it easy to mix well with others similar to themselves. Two Hathors may find that they are in constant competition with one another.

OSIRIS: The Hathor is too sentimental for Osiris. The Hathor seeks close relationships and has a need for firm, emotional commitments. The Osiris feels too restricted by such demands.

OTHER SIGNS

HORUS: Horus and Hathor both allow their imaginations a free reign. Consequently, the two signs may behave somewhat irresponsibly when together.

WADJET: The Hathor finds the learned Wadjet of considerable interest. They may, however, distrust the Wadjet's cool, laid-back approach to life.

SEKHMET: Relationships between Hathors and Sekhmets are particularly volatile. They may adore one another, sharing a love of adventure, travel and excitement. When together, however, both can find their emotions too readily stimulated and arguments may result. These signs often share a love/hate relationship.

THE SPHINX: Hathors generally admire the clever Sphinx, whereas Sphinxes often find the romantic Hathor a stimulating companion.

SHU: Shus and Hathors both share an interest in the exotic and unusual aspects of life. Close friendships and relationships are possible, although marriage between these two signs can sometimes suffer due to a lack of practical considerations.

FATE AND FORTUNE

Over the course of the year the Hathor can expect the following influences to affect their lives during the separate Egyptian months:

THOTH 29 AUGUST – 27 SEPTEMBER:

This month can be a time of success, especially in business matters. However, Hathors should avoid locking horns with the influences of this month. They should let things be as they are, rather than how they would wish them to be.

HORUS 28 SEPTEMBER – 27 OCTOBER:

This is the best time of year for a Hathor to take a vacation. Weekends away can be particularly romantic. Business matters or difficult decisions concerning domestic life are best left until the Hathor has their feet more firmly on the ground.

WADJET 28 OCTOBER – 26 NOVEMBER:

Wadjet acts as a message bearer for the Hathor. News received during the early days of this month can result in a new outlook on life for the Hathor. This is also a time well placed for financial and monetary matters.

SEKHMET 27 NOVEMBER – 26 DECEMBER:

At no other time of the year is the Hathor more likely to lose patience than during the month of Sekhmet. Problems in relationships or with close friends or colleagues may occur and as a result of Hathor irritability.

THE SPHINX 27 DECEMBER – 25 JANUARY:

For the Hathor this month is a time of learning. Hathors involved in academic pursuits will find this a particularly fruitful time of the year. Hathors generally will find that solutions to problems will present themselves. Others should respect the Hathor's point of view during the month of the Sphinx – it is often wise, inspired and deeply intuitive.

SHU 26 JANUARY – 24 FEBRUARY:

If there is a lurking problem in the Hathor's life, this is the time of year when it is most likely to erupt. If there are difficulties in relationships, with friends or at work, they are likely to hit a crisis point. If something should end or change this may be the time to act.

ISIS 25 FEBRUARY – 26 MARCH:

The Isis month is especially linked to financial matters as far as the Hathor is concerned. An unexpected windfall is possible. Any new enterprise initiated during this cycle is likely to reap rewards.

OSIRIS 27 MARCH – 25 APRIL:

Hathors will often find that others rely on them during this month. Most Hathors like attention and are helpful by nature. However, they may find that they are restricted by the constant demands of others.

AMUN 26 APRIL – 25 MAY:

Amun is a sign of authority. Many Hathors distrust authority and especially hate being ordered around. This is a month where the Hathor may find greatest difficulty. Someone close to the Hathor could attempt to persuade them to act against their wishes. The Hathor should stand firm, although avoid becoming entangled in arguments and quarrels.

HATHOR 26 MAY – 24 JUNE:

During the month of their own sign Hathors are in their imaginative element. New ideas are forever occurring to them and fresh possibilities are eagerly grasped. This is a particularly favourable time for anything to do with music or the arts.

THE PHOENIX 25 JUNE – 24 JULY:

In legend the Phoenix continually rose from the ashes. The Phoenix month is a time for new opportunities for the Hathor. Something long awaited may come to fruition. New friendships or relationships are possible. Sport and leisure activities, even games of chance, are favourable for the Hathor at this time.

ANUBIS 25 JULY – 28 AUGUST:

The imaginative and adventurous Hathor is well placed for romance during the month of Anubis. An existing partnership is likely to be enhanced by new prospects, particularly concerning domestic matters and the home. A Hathor on the lookout for a new partner may be pleasantly surprised. New acquaintances and friendships are possible.

HATHOR CORRESPONDENCES

STONE	JASPER (GREEN OR BROWN)
TREE	ELM
FOOD	OLIVE
HERB	FENNEL
FLOWER	COWSLIP

COLOUR	OCHRE
LUCKY NUMBER	10
INCENSE	PATCHOULI
ANIMAL	COW
SYMBOL	

FAMOUS HATHORS

Courtney Cox, Johnny Depp, Joseph Fiennes, Angelina Jolie, Nicole Kidman, Alannis Morissette, Natalie Portman, Mark Wahlberg, Prince William, Noah Wylie.

HATHOR WORKING

O Hathor, Lady Het-Hert
Joyful Goddess of Love, Music and Dance
I call upon thee
Protect me from all ills that approach from the east.
O Hathor, Lady of the Universe
Protect me from all ills that approach from the south.
Het-Hert, Keeper of the Scarab Crown
Protect me from all ills that approach from the west.
O Hathor, Lady of the House of Jubilation
Protect me from all ills that approach from the north.
Great Lady, Daughter of the Night
Remain at all times about me.
Ta-senet-neferti, Ta-senet-neferti.
Lady of Eternal Love
When I cannot hear, lead me.
O Hathor, Child of the Silver Voice
When I cannot see, show me the way.
Het-Hert, Singer of Sweet Desert Songs
Let me recognize and seize the opportunities that
*   I am granted.*
Great Goddess, Mother of Light, Diamond of the Solar Disc
Let thy hand work through me.
Guide me to my path of destiny.
Grant me now thy power.
Ta-senet-neferti, Ta-senet-neferti.

CHAPTER 11

· THE PHOENIX ·

25 JUNE–24 JULY

I have gone forth as a Phoenix, Lord of jubilees, risen and shining.

From a tomb inscription in the Valley of the Kings.

This sacred firebird, known to the Ancient Egyptians as the 'Benu', was a symbol of life and rebirth. In legend this exotic bird made its nest of spices and when the sun's rays set it alight the Phoenix was burned to cinders. A few days later a new Phoenix was born, rising majestically from the ashes of the old. The main characteristic of those born in the sign of the Phoenix is the ability to create possibilities from very little. They are optimistic in the extreme, seldom accepting anything as hopeless. Usually able to find some good even in their worst enemies, the Phoenix is remarkably resilient. They have a close affinity with nature and are often conservationists and vegetarians.

Travel has enormous appeal for the Phoenix, who usually likes secluded places. Hot climates are preferred – winter holidays are not for them. Born in the sign of the firebird, the Phoenix dislikes the cold intensely. Conversely, they can function well in even the worst of heat waves, rushing around busily while others are sweltering. Hot or spicy foods are also a favourite for the Phoenix. Preferring to be active, general television programmes or casual reading are not high on the Phoenix list of priorities. The exceptions are sport or game shows, which the Phoenix may follow with zeal.

The Phoenix has tremendous vitality. Life is an adventure for the Phoenix, although a craving for excitement may lead to tricky situations. Always eager for new experiences, and ready to rise to the challenge, the Phoenix life is full of surprises. So much do they endeavour to fill their lives with excitement, sometimes they forget about the smaller, more practical matters of life. Others may be content to wait for opportunities to arise; Phoenixes will create their own. Indeed, they consider it their personal responsibility to seek out new and interesting possibilities.

POSITIVE CHARACTERISTICS

Resilient, optimistic and determined, the Phoenix has an inventive and adaptable personality. They are industrious and highly active, with the ability to find new uses for the most unlikely things. Technically gifted regarding the crafts, the Phoenix has a conscientious attitude to work. There is a strong tendency to champion the plight of the unfortunate, and an enviable power to inspire confidence and enthusiasm in others.

NEGATIVE CHARACTERISTICS

The Phoenix has a stubborn streak. They prefer to do things their own way – even when they know they are wrong. Often a dreamer, the Phoenix may refuse to face reality when problems occur. Too much time is spent on failed endeavours when the best course of action would be to move on to something else. The Phoenix is often headstrong and occasionally egotistical.

APPEARANCE

Those born in this sign often have a determined appearance. Their intense eyes are extremely attractive to the opposite sex. The Phoenix's nose is usually sharp, although the chin tends to be round. Weight is seldom a problem: an abundance of nervous energy generally keeps the Phoenix slim and agile. Many born in this sign have a cheeky demeanour. Phoenix men may have a rugged look, while the Phoenix woman often has a mischievous smile.

HEALTH

The Phoenix usually enjoys good health, although skin complaints may be a problem. More often than not, this is the result of stress. Diet is seldom a cause of concern for the Phoenix. They can eat almost anything without detriment. Back problems may be in evidence due to a tendency to stoop. The Phoenix is a symbol of vitality and those born in this cycle are usually fit and trim.

WORDS OF ADVICE

Once Phoenixes have made up their minds, they are firm in their convictions. The Phoenix, however, is a sign of action rather than words, and handling a skilled debate is something those born in this cycle find hard. When faced with opposition, the Phoenix generally loses patience, brushing off adverse opinion with an exasperated shrug. Few Phoenixes spend time consulting with others, and are apt to jump to conclusions far too quickly. They sometimes lack sound judgement, although they more than compensate by an abundance of willpower. Most problems the Phoenix encounters arise from an inability to see things from someone else's point of view. Although they are sympathetic to those in obvious distress, they are usually so wrapped up in their own affairs that they take little interest in the opinions of others. Phoenixes should listen to those around them before arriving at conclusions.

SUITABLE OCCUPATIONS

With an adventurous temperament, the Phoenix is especially suited for hazardous occupations. Whether manual or white-collar workers, the Phoenix is generally most successful when self-employed. Few Phoenixes work well with money and so financial careers are best left to others. Phoenix enthusiasm is contagious and a career in sales or promotional work can be highly successful. Technically gifted, those born in this sign make excellent mechanics and engineers.

THE PHOENIX AT WORK

Happiest when working alone, the Phoenix is unlikely to make a success of a business partnership. In any working environment, if colleagues are prepared to let the Phoenix do things their own way positive results often follow. Phoenixes make tough but fair employers, although they may drive their employees a little too hard. As an employee, the Phoenix has optimism that is always a valuable contribution to any workforce. Sometimes, however, their optimism may prove frustrating, particularly if an enterprise is an obvious failure. The Phoenix just doesn't know when to quit.

THE PHOENIX WOMAN

The self-reliant Phoenix makes an excellent career woman. If a housewife she will probably need an outside interest. Invariably, the Phoenix woman is at her best when dividing her talents equally between domestic and business affairs. Possessing an abundance of energy, she can easily handle both. The Phoenix woman has a masculine streak and often prefers the company of men. Phoenix femininity is more commanding than sensual, although there is no lack of romance in her life. As most Phoenix women are able to hold their own in a male environment, a man's reaction is either one of admiration or irritation. Few can simply take-or-leave a Phoenix woman.

The Phoenix woman is seldom jealous. If her partner appears interested in someone else, she usually knows precisely what to do. If she fails, her response is generally to feel that he is not worth the bother. Her partner is expected to work at the relationship – if he fails her, the Phoenix woman will soon look elsewhere. In love, like in most areas of her life, if something is not working out she is inclined to make a clean break and quickly start again.

THE PHOENIX MAN

The Phoenix is more accident prone than many signs, often due to haste rather than carelessness. The Phoenix man is usually more hasty than his female counterpart. Although he is often preoccupied with the safety of others, he tends to disregard such precautions himself. The Phoenix is a skilled craftsman and will usually attempt to rectify a household fault before calling an expert. Stubbornly, when the problem is beyond his scope, he refuses to quit, only to make matters worse.

The Phoenix man is impossible to drag away from anything he is involved in, and his partner needs repeatedly to call him to meals. If he is doing the cooking, however, it's another story altogether. The Phoenix man is the first to lose patience when someone else is late.

Wildly enthusiastic about whoever or whatever is the focus of his attention, the Phoenix seems oblivious to anyone or anything else.

THE PHOENIX PARENT

Phoenix parents usually expect their children to share their own interests, and are often disappointed in this respect. They look after their children well but sometimes expect too much. They are rather too eager to tell them how to run their lives. Phoenix parents are not strict or overbearing by nature – they just want their children to be like them. Phoenixes are usually concerned parents and offer their children considerable encouragement.

THE PHOENIX CHILD

In legend the Phoenix was reborn in the heart of the desert. Like the firebird, Phoenix children are happy to spend time in seclusion. They are certainly not shy or reclusive: they are just content to play alone. The Phoenix child can be a handful for parents and teachers alike. Right from infancy, the Phoenix makes it very clear they have a will of their own. Boisterous in play, they may be given to tantrums if they fail to get their own way. They are at their best when given liberty to think and act for themselves.

The competitive Phoenix spirit emerges in childhood, and most children born in this sign are keen to do well. Although many are good at sport, few succeed in team events. Individual events are best for the Phoenix child, who often excels at athletics or swimming. Phoenix children are not particularly good at taking care of their possessions and a careless streak can result in many a broken toy. The Phoenix boy is unafraid to tackle a child older or bigger than himself. Sometimes this leads to brawls. The Phoenix girl is a tomboy, preferring the company of boys to other girls.

THE PHOENIX FRIEND

The Phoenix is one of the most robust of signs and those born in this cycle have resilient personalities. They will not let the opinions of others deter or influence their actions, and they will completely ignore sneers or cruel remarks if something has failed.

Courageous by nature, the Phoenix is always ready to take risks for their friends. The Phoenix is good in a crisis, usually the first to suggest a solution. Even if something seems hopeless, the Phoenix is an excellent companion to keep things calm. In times of peril the Phoenix will endanger themselves for the good of others, and in war they are often those decorated for feats of heroism.

Although they see the best in most people, Phoenixes dislike arrogance and hate aggression. They are kind and sympathetic to those who are shy or in distress; it is often the Phoenix who comes to the aid of those in trouble. Phoenixes make excellent companions for anyone prepared to take a back seat now and again. They are never boring to be around, but their need for occasional solitude can sometimes be taken the wrong way.

THE PHOENIX PARTNER

Phoenixes will speak their minds frankly, making their motives and objectives clear. Most signs know where they stand with the Phoenix. Tact is not a Phoenix attribute, however, and those of this sign tend to be forthright and outspoken. They seldom lose their temper, although irritability is the usual Phoenix response to someone who has failed to understand their motives. Phoenixes sometimes say more than is wise, and find it difficult to apologize if they have offended without intent. Their usual form of apology is to make up for it in some way without ever saying they are actually sorry.

Not particularly sensual in love, the Phoenix may appear restrained in a relationship. However, they are kind and generous. The Phoenix may be a passionate lover, but romantic small talk is beyond their scope.

Because of their impetuous nature, the Phoenix can fall in love at first sight. They seldom dwell too long on any decision. Actions speak louder than words for the lover born in this sign, and many rush too readily into marriage. So long as the choice is right, however, relationships can be long-lasting. Phoenixes make ideal partners as they hate domestic strife. They would rather give way to their partner's demands than create a fuss. There is usually too much else on their minds for them to become entangled in a quarrel.

THE PHOENIX AND OTHER SIGNS

AFFINITY SIGNS
SHU: The Phoenix gets on best with those who are less active than they. Many born in the Shu sign are calm and serene – at least outwardly. Accordingly, they can exert a positive influence on the Phoenix's impulsive nature.

ISIS: In legend, once reborn, the Phoenix was impelled to fly to the temple of Heliopolis. Like the mythical bird, those born in the

Phoenix sign will find themselves attracted to the exotic or unusual. Isis is perhaps the most intriguing of signs, and their idiosyncratic style is irresistible to the Phoenix.

THOTH: Thoth is a mood-swinger and their behaviour can be erratic. Unlike many signs, the Phoenix is almost impervious to the emotional swings of others. As both the Phoenix and the Thoth need their own space, they make excellent partners and long-lasting relationships are possible.

HATHOR: The Phoenix particularly likes the company of the Hathor. They have a romantic temperament that the Phoenix finds inspiring.

PROBLEM SIGNS

HORUS: Potentially the most problematic sign for the Phoenix is the Horus. The Phoenix can recover from most failures, but the Horus finds it hard. Both signs are adventurous, but when the Phoenix burned to ashes it rose again. The two signs get on great to begin with, but should problems occur the Phoenix cannot understand the Horus's inability to cope.

AMUN and WADJET: Wadjet and Amun are generally signs where the Phoenix finds great difficulty. Both leadership signs, they enjoy taking charge far too much for the Phoenix's liking.

OTHER SIGNS

OSIRIS: The Phoenix and the Osiris often work well together, although in relationships the Phoenix usually seeks consistency generally lacking in the Osiris's life.

SEKHMET: Both Sekhmet and the Phoenix are signs of extreme optimism, and the two get on like a house on fire; after all, they are both creatures of fire. Unfortunately, the restraining elements of other signs is needed by both. When alone together the Phoenix and the Sekhmet can find themselves in adverse situations that are difficult to remedy.

THE PHOENIX: Two Phoenixes work well together but, like two Sekhmets, problems can arise through too little care or planning.

ANUBIS: Phoenixes find the Anubis too pragmatic. These signs seldom mix well as close companions, although on a superficial level there are few problems.

THE SPHINX: The Phoenix dislike of financial matters is well compensated by the Sphinx. The Sphinx is both conservative and thrifty in their approach to most endeavours, and the Phoenix respects such attributes in others.

FATE AND FORTUNE

Over the course of the year the Phoenix can expect the following influences to affect their lives during the separate Egyptian months:

THOTH 29 AUGUST – 27 SEPTEMBER:

Thoth brings imaginative and fresh ideas to the Phoenix mind. New notions conceived during this month are likely to be well founded. At this time of the year the Phoenix tends to make sound decisions.

HORUS 28 SEPTEMBER – 27 OCTOBER:

The Phoenix should be more careful during the Horus month than at any other time. Both are signs of risks taken courageously. The Horus will walk where angels fear to tread, while the Phoenix has little fear of failure. Combined, these influences are apt to leave the Phoenix wide open to rash decisions.

WADJET 28 OCTOBER – 26 NOVEMBER:

As a sign of wisdom, Wadjet will balance Phoenix impetuousness. This can be an especially favourable time for complicated matters previously unresolved. Sporting activities are particularly favoured for the Phoenix during this month. Surprise news can also be expected.

SEKHMET 27 NOVEMBER – 26 DECEMBER:

Both the Phoenix and Sekhmet are creatures of fire. During this month Phoenix imagination will be at its most effective. Most projects are likely to succeed due to the quick reactions of the Phoenix. Relationships or friendships may suffer, however, as the Phoenix may be particularly argumentative at this time of the year.

THE SPHINX 27 DECEMBER – 25 JANUARY:

The Sphinx month can be a period of stagnation for the Phoenix. If things do not seem to be moving ahead as quickly as the Phoenix hoped, matters should be given a little more time.

SHU 26 JANUARY – 24 FEBRUARY:

Very often the Phoenix will be in their element during a Shu month. Normal practical restraints will be lifted by the influence of Shu and the firebird is free to soar to new heights. Romantic, financial and leisure activities are all favourably placed. This is a month of good luck in matters of chance or lottery.

ISIS 25 FEBRUARY – 26 MARCH:

The Phoenix should be prepared for an unexpected meeting with an old acquaintance. This may open a completely new chapter in the Phoenix's life.

OSIRIS 27 MARCH – 25 APRIL:

Romantic disappointments are possible, although it is a particularly favourable month for financial affairs. New opportunities often arise during the Osiris month for the Phoenix, while long-standing projects may end. This is very much a month of change.

AMUN 26 APRIL – 25 MAY:

A combination of the assertive Amun and the determined Phoenix is favourable for business matters. It is especially a time of good fortune in financial affairs. Conversely, it is not a particularly romantic period for the Phoenix. Difficulties in relationships are possible due to distractions and preoccupations.

HATHOR 26 MAY – 24 JUNE:

During this cycle the Phoenix should try to keep their imagination under control. There is a tendency to forge ahead far too quickly. A cautious approach to most endeavours is advised. Any Phoenix seeking love or romance, however, may be pleasantly surprised at this time of the year.

THE PHOENIX 25 JUNE – 24 JULY:

Some signs fare well during their own month and the Phoenix is one such sign. It is a favourable time for travel, change of location or employment. Good news, especially by mail, can be expected.

ANUBIS 25 JULY – 28 AUGUST:

For the Phoenix, the Anubis month can be a time of relative tranquillity. Few Phoenixes are quiet or reserved by nature and impatience may result. Many Phoenixes will find themselves especially frustrated by humdrum, everyday events. This is a good time to take a break. Vacations and leisure activities are favourably placed.

PHOENIX CORRESPONDENCES

STONE	AMBER
TREE	ALDER
FOOD	DATE
SPICE	NUTMEG
FLOWER	DAFFODIL

COLOUR	INDIGO
LUCKY NUMBER	12
INCENSE	SAFFRON
ANIMAL	LYREBIRD
SYMBOL	

FAMOUS PHOENIXES
Kevin Bacon, Tom Cruise, John Cusack, Tom Hanks, Cheryl Ladd,
Liv Tyler.

PHOENIX WORKING

O Benu,
Bird Who Rises from the Flames
I call upon thee
Protect me from all ills that approach from the east.
O Benu, Keeper of the Eternal Fire
Protect me from all ills that approach from the south.
Phoenix, Guardian of the Sacred Persea Tree
Protect me from all ills that approach from the west.
Sun Bird of the Rising Disc
Protect me from all ills that approach from the north.
O Benu, Sacred to the Sun God
Remain at all times about me.
Nefer-Benu-Tchafu-Nes, Nefer-Benu-Tchafu-Nes.
Beautiful Bird of Burning Flames
When I cannot hear, lead me.
O Benu, Divine and Most Holy Bird
When I cannot see, show me the way.
Benu, Who Comes Forth From the Ashes
Let me recognize and seize the opportunities that
   I am granted.
O Benu, Lord of Heliopolis, City of the Sun
Let thy hand work through me.
Guide me to my path of destiny.
Grant me now thy power.
Nefer-Benu-Tchafu-Nes, Nefer-Benu-Tchafu-Nes.

CHAPTER 12

· ANUBIS ·
25 JULY–28 AUGUST

*O Anubis, Lord of the hallowed land, weigh
my soul at the time of my crossing.*

From the Egyptian Book of the Dead.

The jackal-headed god Anubis, known in Ancient Egypt as Anpu,
was the guardian of the underworld and the judge of souls. Those
born in this sign can be creative and imaginative, yet retain a firm
interest in practical affairs. They may be business people or artists,
yet whichever profession they choose both attributes are brought
into play. This is probably the most determined of all the signs.

The Anubis is self-assured in most situations and a natural capacity to take control affords them much respect. The Anubis has an air of authority but is quite prepared to work behind the scenes. To those born in this sign it is the task that is important, not by whom or how it is achieved.

For the Anubis everything has its place. There is a time for work, a time for rest and a time for play. They commit themselves fully to each, but hate to mix the three. Anubis people will devote themselves exclusively to whatever they are doing. They enjoy routine and keep regular habits. The Anubis has a marvellous capacity to work hard all day but once they have knocked off for the evening their minds are tuned exclusively to relaxation. Unless they have something specific to do, the Anubis is content to sit for hours, watching television, reading a book or listening to music.

The Anubis is unafraid of failure or recrimination and is quite prepared to be disbelieved, even ridiculed, until their point is proven. Insults or sneers have little influence on the Anubis, having the confidence and self-assurance to believe they are right. Indeed, Anubis people seldom commit themselves to any enterprise of which they are uncertain. Those born in this cycle are prepared to persevere long and hard to achieve results.

POSITIVE CHARACTERISTICS

Anubis people have a determined spirit with much capacity for creative thinking. They share a sympathetic and hospitable personality and spiritual aspirations are usually well developed. The Anubis has a generous nature and an idealistic attitude to life. The common good is usually a high priority for Anubis who is prepared to make many a personal sacrifice to help those around them. Many have a philosophical attitude to life and most have faith that good will ultimately triumph.

NEGATIVE CHARACTERISTICS

Relationships are sometimes made difficult by an obstinate spirit. There is a marked tendency to disregard the attitudes of others or offend without intent. The Anubis needs to consider every angle of a problem, which so often leads to too much preparation and not enough action. Frequently, Anubis people fail to seize opportunities offered them on a plate.

APPEARANCE

The Anubis gaze is direct and benevolent. They have a habit of nodding knowingly when listening and adopt an understanding smile – even when they are in complete disagreement. Anubis people move with an air of confidence, they carry their heads high and walk with their backs straight. At rest, however, Anubis tends to sprawl.

HEALTH

The Anubis ability to relax completely may result in weight problems. Few Anubis people are worriers, and those born in this cycle are seldom concerned about their own well-being. Many are therefore inclined to ignore preventative medicine or disregard any telltale signs of illness. Repetitive strain injuries, or others such ailments that are best tackled early, may be left unattended by the Anubis. This can lead to complications that might easily have been avoided.

WORDS OF ADVICE

Anubis was the guardian of the netherworld. Like their mythical counterpart, those born in this sign are protective by nature. Once something is theirs they just hate to give it up. Anubis people will adhere to a notion or continue with an enterprise even when it is outmoded or doomed to failure. They should take time to re-examine their circumstances and adjust their approach when necessary. As the Anubis considers every factor before embarking on an enterprise, most endeavours are likely to succeed. If failure does result through unforeseen circumstances, however, the Anubis is usually ill prepared. To avoid being left stranded, Anubis people should remember to keep something in reserve.

SUITABLE OCCUPATIONS

Anubis people flourish in many trades and professions. As keen planners and organizers they fare particularly well in commerce. An artistic Anubis has tremendous insight into what is popular; advertising and the world of fashion employs many an Anubis in important positions. Anubis people are equally content to work behind the scenes. In the world of entertainment, for instance, as many Anubis people are found off-stage as in the public eye. Those Anubis people who do perform before an audience usually do so in a unique and unusual way. Anubis people in manual trades love to see an enterprise develop through every stage to completion. They are keen to witness the result of their contribution; so few Anubis people are comfortable in a closed working environment.

THE ANUBIS AT WORK

The Anubis makes a considerate employer, exercising authority without becoming demonstrative or overbearing. They are always concerned for the well being of their staff, and make certain that they are kept duly informed concerning all aspects of their work. Although Anubis people make excellent bosses, they are not the best of entrepreneurs. In management, the Anubis lacks the ruthless streak sometimes necessary to make financially sound decisions. Concern for their workforce is likely to preside over interests of sheer profit. As employees, Anubis people make a positive contribution to the workforce. They are, however, inclined to side with those in difficulty, and the Anubis's willingness to defend an unpopular workmate can result in friction with other members of staff.

THE ANUBIS WOMAN

Anubis people are sophisticated dressers, although they may be given to some rather unusual styles. Few women born in this cycle blindly follow fashion; they are usually trendsetters rather than followers. They are certainly not conservative in dress, although they go for quality of clothing rather than variety, often preferring darker colours.

The Anubis woman is the most composed of any sign. She is assured, debonair, calm and collected, although not arrogant or aloof. Women born in some signs may need to deliberately make their mark – to the Anubis woman, panache comes naturally. Although the Anubis woman is not flirtatious, she enjoys the attention of men. A certain intangible mystique turns many an eye in her direction.

Women born in this cycle are seldom loners, and most enjoy being part of a group. The Anubis woman likes to stand out in a crowd – not to stand alone. The one thing an Anubis woman cannot stand, however, is male chauvinism. She expects to be treated as an equal, and quickly finds an excuse to leave the company of the condescending male. Moreover, she hates seeing other women dominated by overbearing men. The Anubis woman is the first to offer support to a friend who finds herself the victim of male aggression.

As a career woman, Anubis can be the most successful of signs. However, the Anubis woman likes to devote herself exclusively to whatever she is doing. Few born in this cycle have the desire to continue work once they have started a family.

THE ANUBIS MAN

The mythical Anubis was a guardian, and men born in this cycle have strong family ties. They are proud of their homes and of their family's achievements. They are the perfect providers but like their wives to concentrate on domestic affairs. The Anubis man may treat women well, but expects his partner's place to be in the home. Once settled, Anubis men like to keep their home environment apart from the rest of their lives. At work Anubis is a working man, at home he is a family man. He dedicates himself to each with equal commitment but hates to mix the two.

The Anubis man is a collector of mementoes and memorabilia. In particular, he loves to keep a record of his life, and is often a keen photographer or camcorder enthusiast. He is also a hobbyist, and most Anubis men have a pet interest to occupy their spare time. They work, rest and play – but all have a set place and time. Sunday afternoon, for example, may be set aside for the gardening, a trip in the country or some other specific commitment. Beware of arriving at the Anubis man's home unannounced – he will be most put out if his routine is disturbed. Make sure Anubis has adequate warning of anything that may disrupt his life or necessitate a change of plan.

THE ANUBIS PARENT

The Anubis parent is inclined to be overprotective of their children. They are worriers, who always want to know where their offspring are and what they're up to. Although this is an admirable quality for parents of younger children, when they reach their teens it can be somewhat restricting for the child, and conflicts are likely to arise. The parents of other signs may be prepared to let their teenage children stay over at friends or go to parties and get back late, but the Anubis parent is more likely to keep their offspring grounded or impose strict curfews. They are very proud of their children, and are prone to stick up for them if there are disagreements with teachers. Conflicts are therefore a possibility with school authorities. Anubis parents can be blind to faults in their children, and they have a tendency to react strongly if others dare to criticize their offspring. They want to shield their children from life's traumas.

THE ANUBIS CHILD

Most Anubis children are relaxed in adult company, which some grown-ups may find disconcerting. They mature early and seldom act the fool. From a very early age Anubis children exhibit a responsible and conscientious attitude to life. Anubis children work well in class but hate doing homework. Like their adult counterparts, they feel that once the working day is ended it is time to relax. Revising does not come easily, so examinations may suffer. If they enter higher education, however, the regulated Anubis life style can prove extremely useful. Unlike some students who may skip lectures, the Anubis will attend college conscientiously, as if they were already employed and paid to do a job.

THE ANUBIS FRIEND

Loyalty is an Anubis virtue that remains undaunted in the face of crisis. Anubis people will be especially staunch on a friend's behalf. They are idealists, always ready to come to the aid of others. Anubis people handle criticism well and seldom take offence. Accordingly, they make easy-going friends, especially for those who are outspoken or temperamental. Excitability, erratic behaviour or changes of mood are easily taken in Anubis's stride. All the Anubis asks of their friends is fairness and honesty. Anubis people seldom hold a grudge and are quick to forgive.

Anubis people do not show particularly sound judgement regarding those around them, however. They live as if in an ideal world and believe that others will act as considerately as they. Sadly, the world is not a perfect place and many Anubis people suffer disappointments in business and personal relationships.

A prime Anubis fault is a devotion to schedule. If the Anubis's timetable life is disturbed they are completely thrown. You will not always know when the obliging Anubis is upset. They may agree with your plans to disrupt their routine, only to spend the rest of the day repeatedly looking at their watch.

THE ANUBIS PARTNER

The Anubis is affectionate and protective, although not romantic by nature. Those born in this sign look for home comforts in a relationship rather than matrimonial bliss. Both Anubis men and women seek partners who are homely and consistent. Anubis men seek devoted, domesticated wives, and Anubis women seek steady, reliable husbands.

Anubis people throw themselves completely into a relationship and expect their partners to do the same. This, of course, will not always be so, particularly in the early days of dating. Such premature Anubis expectations are sometimes disturbing to those of other signs who may need longer to make firm commitments. If the

Anubis was not so impatient to marry and settle down, many a failed relationship might have developed quite differently. Anubis people should always remember that partners often need more time.

ANUBIS AND OTHER SIGNS

AFFINITY SIGNS

THOTH: The Anubis works particularly well with the Thoth. Thoth imagination can develop the Anubis's more practical ideas and both have considerable creativity. The two signs also compliment each other in business matters.

HATHOR: Anubis and Hathor are particularly compatible signs, especially concerning romantic affiliations. Both share common interests, although their personalities are sufficiently different not to clash.

SHU: The Anubis's strong family ties and protective instincts can make them ideal partners for Shus. Shus often look at life from a very different perspective to the Anubis and their romantic imagination usually aids the Anubis's creativity.

OSIRIS: Anubis people are prepared to give others their own space – something the Osiris desperately needs. Unlike some signs, the Anubis is usually an open book, having no problem with Osiris inquisitiveness.

PROBLEM SIGNS

ANUBIS: Anubis people often get on well with Anubis people of their own sex. Romantic relationships may suffer, however. Anubis women find Anubis men far too chauvinistic regarding their ideas of marriage.

SEKHMET: Sekhmets and Anubis people share similar creativity. However, the headstrong Anubis can often clash with the fiery temperament of the Sekhmet. Neither is prepared to give way to the other.

THE SPHINX: Those born in the Sphinx and Anubis signs often experience a clash of interests and personalities. Sometimes they may even distrust one another.

ISIS: The Isis can unnerve the Anubis. Few Anubis people like ideas as unconventional as those many born in the sign of Isis appear to display.

OTHER SIGNS

THE PHOENIX: Phoenixes find Anubis people too pragmatic. Although on a superficial level these two signs may tolerate one other, they seldom mix well as close companions.

AMUN: Anubis people and Amuns mix well socially as both are polite and confident signs. When working together, however, there can be clashes of interest. In marriage, there may be problems as both signs are exceptionally stubborn.

HORUS: The Anubis and the Horus have few problems socially, although the Horus is seldom prepared to make the sort of long-term commitments the Anubis expects.

WADJET: Anubis people like to know precisely where they stand and so find the Wadjet difficult to fathom.

FATE AND FORTUNE

Over the course of the year the Anubis can expect the following influences to affect their lives during the separate Egyptian months:

THOTH 29 AUGUST – 27 SEPTEMBER :

For any Anubis in need of a vacation, now is the ideal time to get away. This is also the perfect month for romance.

HORUS 28 SEPTEMBER – 27 OCTOBER:

In the month of Horus, Anubis people may profit by ignoring their usual reticence concerning risk ventures. It is a month of luck in matters of chance.

WADJET 28 OCTOBER – 26 NOVEMBER:

Wadjet is a sign of sudden or unexpected news for the Anubis. During this month Anubis may be taken completely by surprise. For any Anubis seeking new friendships or partnerships this can be an especially favourable time.

SEKHMET 27 NOVEMBER – 26 DECEMBER:

For Anubis the fire-breathing Sekhmet brings imaginative insight. Anubis people are likely to be inspired by new and fruitful ideas. This is a positive time for any change of job or location.

THE SPHINX 27 DECEMBER – 25 JANUARY:

This can be an emotionally trying month for Anubis. It is not the best time for important practical or romantic decisions.

SHU 26 JANUARY – 24 FEBRUARY:

The Shu month is often the most uneventful in the Anubis's year. The god of the air is normally way out of reach for Anubis – so also are progress and opportunity.

ISIS 25 FEBRUARY – 26 MARCH:

Many Anubis people find that the Isis month brings luck and welcome news. It is a time of good fortune for many born in the Anubis sign.

OSIRIS 27 MARCH – 25 APRIL:

The Anubis is often frustrated by acquaintances who are not as far-sighted as they. During the elusive Osiris month this can be particularly true. Anubis people may find it especially hard to convince others of their ideas or point of view.

AMUN 26 APRIL – 25 MAY:

Amun and Anubis are both signs favourable for business and enterprise. In financial matters the Anubis is often at their best during an Amun month. It is a time when hard work and dedication may finally pay off.

HATHOR 26 MAY – 24 JUNE:

New friendships or relationships are possible and old acquaintances may be renewed. Few Anubis people have problems during a Hathor month. Even if difficulties should arise, Anubis people are well placed to handle problems that befall them.

THE PHOENIX 25 JUNE – 24 JULY:

The influence of the fiery Phoenix may result in headstrong actions for the Anubis. They should take care about saying more than they should, lest they offend without intent.

ANUBIS 25 JULY – 28 AUGUST:

The Anubis works well during their own month, although friendships and relationships may suffer. Anubis people could find themselves having to work so hard that they exclude their loved ones from their busy schedule.

ANUBIS CORRESPONDENCES

STONE   OBSIDIAN

TREE   YEW

FOOD   APPLE

HERB   SAVORY

FLOWER   FOXGLOVE

COLOUR   BLACK

LUCKY NUMBER   3

INCENSE   KYPHI

ANIMAL   JACKAL

SYMBOL

FAMOUS ANUBISES

Ben Affleck, Gillian Anderson, Antonio Banderas, Halle Berry, Sandra Bullock, David Duchovny, Melanie Griffith, Lisa Kudrow, Matt Le Blanc, Jennifer Lopez, H.P. Lovecraft, Matthew Perry, River Phoenix, J.K. Rowling, Kevin Spacey, Charlize Theron.

ANUBIS WORKING

O Anubis, Mighty Anpu
Jackal God of the Sacred Land
I call upon thee
Protect me from all ills that approach from the east.
O Anubis, Dweller in the Halls of Time
Protect me from all ills that approach from the south.
Anpu, Guardian at the Gates of Dawn
Protect me from all ills that approach from the west.
Api-Abu, Counter of Hearts
Protect me from all ills that approach from the north.
Anpu, Power of the Light Within the Caves
Remain at all times about me.
Khenti-seh-neter, Khenti-seh-neter.
He who Presides over the God's Pavilion
When I cannot hear, lead me.
Anpu, Light of the Two Worlds
When I cannot see, show me the way.
O Anubis, Whose Face is Golden as the Day
Let me recognize and seize the opportunities that
*   I am granted.*
O Anubis, Protector of Valiant Kings,
Let thy hand work through me.
Guide me to my path of destiny.
Grant me now thy power.
Khenti-seh-neter, Khenti-seh-neter.

RESOURCES

The author can be contacted on:
http://www.stormconstantine.com
Magical community on MSN:
http://communities.msn.co.uk/MeoniaMagicandMystery

CLIVE BARRETT

ANCIENT EGYPTIAN TAROT

NEW EDITION

The Ancient Egyptian Tarot returns the Tarot to the land of its ancestors. Based on ancient Egyptian life and mythology, this stunning deck and handbook also includes a history and use of the tarot, which author Clive Barrett believes orginated in Egypt.

The Ancient Egyptian Tarot reunites traditional Egyptian symbolism and imagery which occur throughout all tarots with fully researched scenes depicting ancient Egyptian life and mythology.

The Major Arcana's central theme is the story of Osiris and his resurrection by the hands of Isis, while the Minor Arcana reflect the culture of the ancient Egyptians based upon genuine wall paintings and carvings from their tombs and temples.

FIONA HORNE

SEVEN DAYS TO A MAGICKAL NEW YOU

Fiona Horne is a Witch with Attitude – young, beautiful and
extremely funky. Here she shares the secrets of her craft with
this week-long guide to releasing your own inner witch!

This enchanting guide takes you day-by-day on a week-long journey
of magickal transformation. With each day ruled by a different
planet, this little book is packed with fun and practical suggestions,
from breakfast picnics to decorating your own altar. Includes easy
and inspiring ways to bring more magick into your life and enhance
your feelgood factor, including day by day rituals, simple chakra
work, how to make elixirs and other potions.

Fiona takes you right through each day, so you feel good from the
moment you open your eyes to last thing at night. Perfect for
chasing away those workaday blues.

KEITH SEDDON AND JOCELYN ALMOND

A BOOK OF EGYPTIAN RITUAL

THE SEASONAL RITES OF EGYPTIAN PAGANISM
NEW EDITION

A unique workbook of ancient Egyptian rituals from experts in the field.

Providing a fascinating insight into the mysteries of the ancient Egyptian world, this book presents eight seasonal rites for performance at the solstices, equinoxes and cross-quarter days.

These rites are composed entirely of ancient Egyptian religious texts, some as much as 4,300 years old. Made newly accessible to a modern readership, they provide a fascinating insight into the mysteries of the ancient Egyptian world. Includes:

- an introduction to and explanation of each rite
- rites that are ideal for Pagans who may not have a temple
- rites that may be performed at home
- a general overview of ancient Egyptian religious and magical beliefs
- a glossary of the deities' names and Egyptian terms

NEIL SOMERVILLE

YOUR CHINESE HOROSCOPE FOR 2003

The year 2003 is the Chinese Year of the Goat – what will this mean for you? This complete guide contains all the predictions you will need to take you into the 21st century.

Chinese astrology is being rediscovered in the West and is proving to be a highly accurate system of character analysis and prediction. This bestselling guide – now in its 15th year – includes:

- everything you need to know about the 12 signs of the Chinese zodiac
- an explanation of the Five Elements, and which one governs your sign
- individual predictions to help you find love, luck and success

JOSEPH POLANSKY

YOUR PERSONAL HOROSCOPE FOR 2003

THE ONLY ONE-VOLUME HOROSCOPE YOU'LL EVER NEED

Your complete one-volume guide to the year 2003 – the only horoscope you will ever need, with month-by-month forecasts for every sign.

This bestselling one-volume guide gives you individual predictions for the year ahead and shows you how you, your friends, your family and lovers will fare. It includes:

- a month-by-month forecast for every sign
- a personality profile for each sign
- detailed predictions of your best days, worst days, and the ideal days to attract love or money